Mercatus Studies ir  /

Series Editors
Virgil Henry Storr
Mercatus Center
George Mason University
Fairfax, VA, USA

Stefanie Haeffele
Mercatus Center
George Mason University
Fairfax, VA, USA

Political economy is a robust field of study that examines the economic and political institutions that shape our interactions with one another. Likewise, social economy focuses on the social interactions, networks, and communities that embody our daily lives. Together, these fields of study seek to understand the historical and contemporary world around us by examining market, political, and social institutions. Through these sectors of life, people come together to exchange goods and services, solve collective problems, and build communities to live better together.

Scholarship in this tradition is alive and thriving today. By using the lens of political and social economy, books in this series will examine complex social problems, the institutions that attempt to solve these problems, and the consequences of action within such institutions. Further, this approach lends itself to a variety of methods, including fieldwork, case studies, and experimental economics. Such analysis allows for deeper understanding of social phenomena, detailing the context, incentives, and interactions that shape our lives. This series provides a much-needed space for interdisciplinary research on contemporary topics on political and social economy. In much of academia today, scholars are encouraged to work independently and within the strict boundaries of their disciplines. However, the pursuit of understanding our society requires social scientists to collaborate across disciplines, using multiple methods. This series provides such an opportunity for scholars interested in breaking down the boundaries of disciplines in order to better understand the world around us.

More information about this series at
http://www.palgrave.com/gp/series/15998

Stefanie Haeffele • Virgil Henry Storr
Editors

Government
Responses to Crisis

palgrave
macmillan

Editors
Stefanie Haeffele
F. A. Hayek Program for Advanced Study in
Philosophy, Politics, and Economics
Mercatus Center at George Mason University
Fairfax, VA, USA

Virgil Henry Storr
F. A. Hayek Program for Advanced Study in
Philosophy, Politics, and Economics
Mercatus Center at George Mason University
Fairfax, VA, USA

Mercatus Studies in Political and Social Economy
ISBN 978-3-030-39308-3   ISBN 978-3-030-39309-0   (eBook)
https://doi.org/10.1007/978-3-030-39309-0

This Palgrave Macmillan imprint is published by the registered company Springer Nature Switzerland AG.
The registered company address is: Gewerbestrasse 11, 6330 Cham, Switzerland

Contents

1   Introduction   1
    Stefanie Haeffele and Virgil Henry Storr

2   The Rules of the Game and Post-Disaster Rebuilding and
    Recovery   13
    Laura E. Grube

3   Government as Gardener: Cultivating the Environment for
    Private Sector Natural Disaster Response   27
    Steven Horwitz

4   The Role of the Local Emergency Manager in a Centralized
    System of Disaster Management   45
    Amy LePore

5   Recognizing Vulnerability and Capacity: Federal Initiatives
    Focused on Children and Youth Across the Disaster
    Lifecycle   61
    Lori Peek and Simone Domingue

6   The Political Economy of Foreign Intervention   89
    Christopher J. Coyne and Garrett Wood

7   When Is Top-Down State-Building Appropriate?   111
    Jennifer Murtazashvili and Ilia Murtazashvili

8   The European Migrant Crisis: A Case Study in Failure of
    Governmental and Supra-governmental Responses   129
    Paul Dragos Aligica and Thomas Savidge

Index   143

List of Contributors

Paul Dragos Aligica F. A. Hayek Program for Advanced Study in Philosophy, Politics, and Economics, Mercatus Center at George Mason University, Fairfax, VA, USA

Christopher J. Coyne Department of Economics, George Mason University, Fairfax, VA, USA
F. A. Hayek Program for Advanced Study in Philosophy, Politics, and Economics, Mercatus Center at George Mason University, Fairfax, VA, USA

Simone Domingue Department of Sociology, University of Colorado Boulder, Boulder, CO, USA
Natural Hazards Center, University of Colorado Boulder, Boulder, CO, USA

Laura E. Grube Department of Economics, Beloit College, Beloit, WI, USA

Stefanie Haeffele F. A. Hayek Program for Advanced Study in Philosophy, Politics, and Economics, Mercatus Center at George Mason University, Fairfax, VA, USA

Steven Horwitz Department of Economics, Ball State University, Muncie, IN, USA

Amy LePore Anthem Planning Inc., Middletown, DE, USA

Ilia Murtazashvili Graduate School of Public and International Affairs, University of Pittsburgh, Pittsburgh, PA, USA

Jennifer Murtazashvili Graduate School of Public and International Affairs, University of Pittsburgh, Pittsburgh, PA, USA

Lori Peek Department of Sociology, University of Colorado Boulder, Boulder, CO, USA
Natural Hazards Center, University of Colorado Boulder, Boulder, CO, USA

Thomas Savidge George Mason University, Fairfax, VA, USA

Virgil Henry Storr Department of Economics, George Mason University, Fairfax, VA, USA
F. A. Hayek Program for Advanced Study in Philosophy, Politics, and Economics, Mercatus Center at George Mason University, Fairfax, VA, USA

Garrett Wood Department of Economics, Virginia Wesleyan University, Virginia Beach, VA, USA

List of Tables

Table 5.1   Examples of static versus dynamic and intersectional
definitions of social vulnerability   67

Table 5.2   Description of federal disaster programs and initiatives
focused on engaging children and youth   70

Table 5.3   Summary of available federal guidance documents for adults
and focused on children, youth, and disasters   74

Table 8.1   Taxonomy of migration factors   133

1

Introduction

Stefanie Haeffele and Virgil Henry Storr

1.1 Introduction

Crises can disrupt lives and devastate communities. Think of the personal crises that regularly plague individuals, like illnesses and unemployment, and challenge families, like the death of a relative or the dissolution of a marriage. Think of crises like severe economic downturns, hyperinflation, debt crises, earthquakes, fires, war, political unrest, riots, and health epidemics that can destroy communities. These crises can be natural (such as hurricanes, tornadoes, and floods), man-made (such as conflict

S. Haeffele (✉)
F. A. Hayek Program for Advanced Study in Philosophy, Politics, and Economics, Mercatus Center at George Mason University, Fairfax, VA, USA
e-mail: shaeffele@mercatus.gmu.edu

V. H. Storr
F. A. Hayek Program for Advanced Study in Philosophy, Politics, and Economics, Mercatus Center at George Mason University, Fairfax, VA, USA

Department of Economics, George Mason University, Fairfax, VA, USA

© The Author(s) 2020   1
S. Haeffele, V. H. Storr (eds.), *Government Responses to Crisis*, Mercatus Studies in Political and Social Economy, https://doi.org/10.1007/978-3-030-39309-0_1

and economic recessions), or, more often than not, a combination of the two (such as the compounding effect of the levees breaking after Hurricane Katrina and the increasing frequency and ferocity of storms due to climate change). While it is certainly the case that wealthier individuals and more developed communities are often better able to respond to crises (see Kahn 2005), every community is vulnerable to crises. Individuals and communities will, thus, thrive or flounder, prosper or struggle, succeed or fail depending in part on whether or not they respond effectively to crises.

Effectively responding to crises, however, can be extremely difficult. In the case of community-level crises, local residents, business owners, and government officials are often directly affected and can experience physical damage and injury as well as mental and emotional distress. Further, in an ever-interconnected world, crises in one geographical location can affect individuals and communities across the globe by affecting their family, friends, and colleagues, by resulting in migration, or by disrupting communication networks and trade routes. And, while everyone in a community may be affected by crises, as noted above, individuals and groups that are marginalized—such as racial and ethnic minorities, women, children, the elderly, people with disabilities, and the poor—are less likely to be able to prepare for and rebound from disaster (see, for instance, Hewitt 1997; Morrow 1999; Cutter et al. 2003; Wisner et al. 2004; Bourque et al. 2007; Phillips et al. 2009; Enarson 2012; Thomas et al. 2013; Peek et al. 2018; Veenema 2018).

Consider, for instance, Hurricane Sandy, which caused considerable damage along the northeast coast of the United States in 2012. The storm caused 73 deaths in the United States, damaged or destroyed over 37,000 primary residences, and resulted in $60 billion in damages.[1] Or, consider, Hurricane Maria, which caused over $90 billion dollars in damages in Puerto Rico, displaced around a hundred thousand residents, and resulted in almost 3000 deaths (although some estimates place the death toll much higher).[2] Recovering from disasters of this scale and scope can be a daunting challenge for disaster survivors. The costs associated with rebuilding after a major disaster can be extremely high. Moreover, the benefits of rebuilding rather than relocating are necessarily uncertain.

Indeed, rebuilding only makes sense if others in the community plan to rebuild and the community is likely to rebound. In this scenario, the rational move for disaster survivors is to wait and see what others do before committing to a particular recovery strategy. Storr et al. (2015) and others have described post-disaster recovery as a collective action problem because rebuilding in the wake of a disaster is only rational if other key community members also rebuild.

Effectively responding to a community-wide crisis, like a hurricane, war, or a prolonged economic recession, means finding ways to overcome these collective action problems that complicate response and recovery. Still, we see individuals and communities rebounding from crises all the time. How do individuals and communities effectively respond to and bounce back after crises? Arguably, effectively responding to crises often requires that affected individuals have, borrow, or attract the requisite resources and that they cooperate and coordinate their activities with one another.

Often individuals and communities rely on bottom-up strategies to respond to crises. Local entrepreneurs provide needed goods and services, community members leverage their social networks, and community leaders drive and coordinate recovery efforts and in the aftermath of crises (Storr et al. 2015). These bottom-up efforts can be critical to individuals and communities as they rebound. But, there are concerns regarding whether or not these bottom-up efforts will ever be adequate responses to crises. Given the scale, scope, and complexities of crises as well as the adverse impact on socially vulnerable populations, it is unsurprising that citizens, media, and policymakers alike turn to governments to take a leading role in response, recovery, and even mitigation and preparedness efforts. Indeed, the public seems to call for increased government intervention and demand higher performance by government organizations after crises (see Kapucu and Van Wart 2006; Chamlee-Wright and Storr 2010a).

This volume examines and advances the literature on governmental responses to crises, describes the lessons learned from past research, and discusses the proper roles, responsibilities, and expectations for government action after crises.

1.2   Understanding the Role of Government in Crisis Response and Recovery Efforts

Large-scale crises—such as hurricanes, famine, war, and severe economic downturns—can cause deaths, injury, and displacement of the population; destroy infrastructure and crops; induce electricity and communication network outages; and lead to shortages in food, gasoline, medicine, and other essential goods. This destruction and displacement can result in tremendous uncertainty for crisis survivors, who must assess how to respond. People may lose their jobs and homes. Additionally, essential services (e.g. education, health care, and welfare programs) may be suspended. Rebounding from crises means either deciding to start fresh somewhere else or deciding to rebuild and reopen damaged or destroyed homes, businesses, and schools. Rebuilding requires not only access to resources but also an understanding that others will do the same so that there are customers to serve, employees to hire, children to educate, and a community to belong. After Hurricane Katrina in 2005, for instance, many residents, journalists, scholars, and politicians worried that New Orleans would never fully recover and that its unique social and cultural impact would become extinct. Similar worries could be said of nations long suffering from civil wars or economic crises, such as Venezuela, Afghanistan, and Somalia. And, these challenges impact not only the residents of these communities but their political leaders as well.

Bottom-up responses to crises can often be effective because local actors often have the requisite knowledge needed to properly assess the specific challenges that must be overcome and the incentives to identify the solutions that best meet the needs of crises survivors. Storr et al. (2015), for instance, identify how local commercial, political, and social entrepreneurs promote disaster recovery by providing needed goods and services, repairing and replacing disrupted social networks, and signaling that disaster recovery is likely to occur and might already be underway. Similarly, Aldrich (2012), Chamlee-Wright and Storr (2010b), and Storr and Haeffele-Balch (2012) have pointed to how community members can access needed information and resources through their social networks. Indeed, social capital has proven to be a critical resource for crisis recovery in a number of different scenarios (see Bolin and Stanford 1998; Hurlbert et al. 2000, 2001; Shaw and Goda 2004; Paton 2007; Chamlee-Wright 2010; Aldrich 2012; Storr et al. 2015). Additionally, Coyne (2008) has proposed that trade rather than top-down post-war reconstruction efforts is likely to be effective in promoting community development in post-war contexts. Big businesses, like Walmart, have been found to aid local communities after disasters (Horwitz 2009). Further, even vulnerable populations such as children (see Peek 2008), the elderly (see Aldrich 2019), and citizens of weak and failed states (see Murtazashvili 2016; Galbraith and Stiles 2006; Bullough et al. 2013) actively participate in community response and recovery efforts.

Although these bottom-up strategies have proven to be robust in the wake of multiple crises, due to the scale, scope, and complexities of crises as well as the collective action problem faced by those affected by crises and hoping to rebound, there is often an expectation that central governments play a key role in crisis management. Specifically, top-down solutions may have an advantage over bottom-up responses to crises in (1) providing needed resources, (2) coordinating and mobilizing response and recovery efforts, (3) responding to crises that were created by or exacerbated by government action, and (4) ensuring that individuals, community leaders, businesses, nonprofits, and local governments have the space to act. Significant resources are often needed to effectively respond to crises. Government may provide personnel to respond to security threats, rescue stranded residents, clear debris, and rebuild infrastructure after a storm; may provide supplies (e.g. water and food), services (e.g. health care), and shelter; and may provide financial assistance to individuals, small business, and state and local governments to rebuild buildings and reestablish utilities and public services. National governments and supranational governmental organizations often have access to a wide variety of public personnel and funding that can aid individuals, communities, and local and state governments. Likewise, coordinating and mobilizing response and recovery efforts often requires being able to communicate across a variety of organizations and prioritizing a myriad of activities. Funneling activity through a central node can help organize activity and take advantage of economies of scale (see Pipa 2006; Tierney 2007; Thaler and Sunstein 2008; Springer 2009; Fakhruddin and Chivakidakarn 2014; Coppola 2015).

Moreover, some crises may be induced or exacerbated by government action and, therefore, require government responses to reduce harms. For instance, when a country goes to war, it must also address the harms imposed on its population during and after the war. Extended war can shift and destroy resources, including turning productive citizens into soldiers and rationing food and materials for military use. Only governments might be in a position to facilitate a return to normalcy in this context.

Finally, governments can help ensure that individuals, private organizations, and civil society have the space to act during and after crises. If bottom-up efforts are critical to effectively responding to crises, then community members must be given the space to coordinate and lead community rebound, to utilize their social capital as well as their skills and expertise, to obtain information about the crisis and the needs of affected residents, and to work with one another to rebound. Government can encourage these efforts by maintaining a stable rule of law, providing funding, and refraining from restricting private action after crises.

While there is a positive role for government during and after crises, government intervention is not without limitations. Specifically, government organizations face challenges identifying and assessing needs and coordinating resources (e.g. government personnel may take days to weeks to arrive and may misallocate supplies). They also face challenges implementing recovery plans that take time to research, compile, and disseminate only to be met with public criticism and even delay recovery (see Sobel and Leeson 2007; Coyne 2008, 2013; Chamlee-Wright 2010; Haeffele-Balch and Storr 2015; Storr et al. 2015). To be effective, government actors must be able to (1) access information about the damage on the ground and the resources needed and available, (2) prioritize and implement response and recovery activities, and (3) adapt to changing circumstances in order to successfully signal and induce recovery (see Sobel and Leeson 2007; Chamlee-Wright 2010; Storr et al. 2015). Given the epistemic position that governments occupy, successfully performing these three roles is a challenge. Additionally, governments are not spared from the effects of crises. They are composed of individuals who are also impacted by crises and face many of the same challenges in identifying needs, prioritizing action, and adjusting to changing circumstances. Political considerations—such electoral competitiveness, partisanship, and reelection concerns—can also alter the implementation and performance of government intervention (see Sobel and Leeson 2006; Schmidtlein et al. 2008; Salkowe and Chakraborty 2009; Reeves 2011; Husted and Nickerson 2014). Given these capabilities and challenges, any government action should be thoughtfully designed, implemented, analyzed, and adjusted in order to determine its proper role in crisis response and recovery.

1.3 Summary of Chapters in the Volume

The chapters in this volume examine the role, expectations, and capabilities of government response and recovery efforts, highlighting the complex nature of crises as well as the limitations and potential of government efforts to stem the varied impacts of crises. Together, these chapters show that government response and recovery efforts are by no means guaranteed to serve their purposes and instead must be designed, implemented, and analyzed with care and humility. The contributors of this volume are accomplished scholars and seasoned practitioners in disaster and crisis studies and management, spanning multiple disciplines, including sociology, economics, and public administration.

The first two chapters focus on the government's role in maintaining, clarifying, and enforcing the "rules of the game" in the post-disaster context. After a disaster, people are faced with a collective action problem, where deciding to rebuild is contingent on the actions of others and where uncertainty abounds. Government can and should play a role in aiding in decision making and reducing uncertainty, Laure E. Grube argues in Chap. 2, by (1) helping to ensure that rules are clear and known in advance, (2) protecting private property rules, and (3) supporting rules that allow local actors to step in. Steven Horwitz, in Chap. 3, argues that government, in an effort to cultivate the environment for a thriving market and civil society, should focus on rules that are known, fairly enforced, and stable by using the principles of "first, doing no harm," "keeping promises," and the decentralization of government authority.

Next, in Chap. 4, Amy LePore explores the role of local emergency managers in an ever more centralized disaster management system. While

the importance of local authority and participation in disaster preparedness, response, and recovery is recognized by the federal government, the
large role that the federal government plays in funding local emergency
management restricts local autonomy. Through a survey of local emergency managers, LePore found that most acknowledge the importance of
local autonomy yet end up still seeking federal funds because they are
necessary for pursuing emergency management functions. If local emergency managers are to have more authority in disaster management, this
tie to federal funds must be reexamined.

In Chap. 5, Lori Peek and Simone Domingue examine how the federal
government has acknowledged the vulnerabilities and capacities of children in the post-disaster context over the past decade. Peek and Domingue
catalog the various federal guidance documents and initiatives for children and those that interact with children (in the home, school, etc.),
which highlight potential vulnerabilities, provide information and awareness, and encourage children to take an active role in preparing for,
responding and recovering from, and mitigating against disasters. They
also identify gaps, such as the lack of guidance documents and programs
that involve children in mitigation and recovery efforts and that approach
the diverse population of children from an intersectionality lens.

The next chapter (Chap. 6), by Christopher J. Coyne and Garrett
Wood, examines the use of foreign intervention in responding to crises
abroad. They argue that governments face several types of constraints
when trying to use force, humanitarian aid, and development and training to intervene in crises occurring in other nations. In particular,
nations face knowledge and incentive problems when trying to influence recovery and establish new governments and institutions in foreign nations.

Yet, there is still a role for top-down state-building in weak and failed
states, argue Jennifer Murtazashvili and Ilia Murtazashvili in Chap. 7.
Government intervention may be beneficial when self-governance breaks
down and when there is economies of scale in producing public goods.
They highlight the importance of polycentric institutions while establishing a proper role of top-down intervention through an examination of
fieldwork in Afghanistan.

And in Chap. 8, Paul Dragos Aligica and Thomas Savidge examine the European Union's (EU's) response to the recent influx of migrants. While the EU is designed to be a polycentric governance structure that allows for coordination among its member states, they argue that Germany's unilateral approach to migration and the subsequent anti-migrant backlash show a failure in the EU's structure to effectively coordinate large-scale, complex, and controversial crises.

Notes

1. These figures are available online at https://www.fema.gov/sandy-recovery-office and https://www.fema.gov/news-release/2013/10/25/year-after-hurricane-sandy-new-jersey-recovery-numbers.
2. These figures are available online at https://coast.noaa.gov/states/fast-facts/hurricane-costs.html and https://www.cnn.com/2018/08/28/health/puerto-rico-gw-report-excess-deaths/index.html.

References

Aldrich, D. 2012. *Building Resilience Social Capital in Post-Disaster Recovery*. Chicago: University of Chicago Press.
———. 2019. *Black Wave: How Networks and Governance Shaped Japan's 3/11 Disasters*. Chicago: University of Chicago Press.
Bolin, R., and L. Stanford. 1998. The Northridge Earthquake: Community-Based Approaches to Unmet Recovery Needs. *Disasters* 22 (1): 21–38.
Bourque, L.B., J.M. Siegel, M. Kano, and M.M. Wood. 2007. Morbidity and Mortality Associated with Disasters. In *Handbook of Disaster Research*, ed. H. Rodríguez, E.L. Quarantelli, and R.R. Dynes, 97–112. New York: Springer.
Bullough, A., M. Renko, and T. Myatt. 2013. Danger Zone Entrepreneurs: The Importance of Resilience and Self-Efficiency for Entrepreneurial Intentions. *Entrepreneurship Theory and Practice* 38 (3): 473–499.
Chamlee-Wright, E. 2010. *The Cultural and Political Economy of Recovery*. New York: Routledge.
Chamlee-Wright, E., and V.H. Storr. 2010a. Expectations of Government's Response to Disaster. *Public Choice* 144 (1–2): 253–274.

————. 2010b. The Role of Social Entrepreneurship in Post-Katrina Recovery. *International Journal of Innovation and Regional Development* 2 (1–2): 149–164.

Coppola, D. 2015. *Introduction to International Disaster Management*. Oxford: Elsevier.

Coyne, C.J. 2008. *After War: The Political Economy of Exporting Democracy*. Stanford: Stanford University Press.

————. 2013. *Doing Bad by Doing Good: Why Humanitarian Action Fails*. Stanford: Stanford University Press.

Cutter, S.L., B.J. Boruff, and W.L. Shirley. 2003. Social Vulnerability to Environmental Hazards. *Social Science Quarterly* 84 (2): 242–261.

Enarson, E. 2012. *Women Confronting Natural Disaster: From Vulnerability to Resilience*. Boulder, CO: Lynne Rienner Publishers.

Fakhruddin, S.H.M., and Y. Chivakidakarn. 2014. A Case Study for Early Warning and Disaster Management in Thailand. *International Journal of Disaster Risk Reduction* 9: 159–180.

Galbraith, C.S., and C.H. Stiles. 2006. Disasters and Entrepreneurship: A Short Review. *International Research in the Business Disciplines* 5: 147–166.

Haeffele-Balch, S., and V.H. Storr. 2015. Austrian Contributions to the Literature on Natural and Unnatural Disasters. In *New Thinking in Austrian Political Economy (Advances in Austrian Economics, Vol. 19)*, ed. C.J. Coyne and V.H. Storr. Bingley, UK: Emerald.

Hewitt, K. 1997. *Regions of Risk: A Geographical Introduction to Disasters*. Boston: Addison Wesley Longman.

Horwitz, S. 2009. Wal-Mart to the Rescue: Private Enterprise's Response to Hurricane Katrina. *The Independent Review* 13 (4): 511–528.

Hurlbert, J., V. Haines, and J. Beggs. 2000. Core Networks and Tie Activation: What Kinds of Routine Networks Allocate Resources in Nonroutine Situations? *American Sociological Review* 65 (4): 598–618.

Hurlbert, J., J. Beggs, and V. Haines. 2001. Social Capital in Extreme Environments. In *Social Capital: Theory and Research*, ed. N. Lin, K. Cook, and R. Burt. New York: Aldine De Gruyter.

Husted, T., and D. Nickerson. 2014. Political Economy of Presidential Disaster Declarations and Federal Disaster Assistance. *Public Finance Review* 42 (1): 35–57.

Kahn, M.E. 2005. The Death Toll from Natural Disasters: The Role of Income, Geography, and Institutions. *Review of Economics and Statistics* 87 (2): 271–284.

Kapucu, N., and M. Van Wart. 2006. The Evolving Role of the Public Sector in Managing Catastrophic Disasters: Lessons Learned. *Administration & Society* 38 (3): 279–308.

Morrow, B.H. 1999. Identifying and Mapping Community Vulnerability. *Disasters* 23 (1): 1–18.

Murtazashvili, J. 2016. *Informal Order and the State in Afghanistan*. New York: Cambridge University Press.

Paton, D. 2007. Preparing for Natural Hazards: The Role of Community Trust. *Disaster Prevention and Management: An International Journal* 16 (3): 370–379.

Peek, L. 2008. Children and Disasters: Understanding Vulnerability, Developing Capacities, and Promoting Resilience. *Children, Youth, and Environments* 18: 1–29.

Peek, L., D. Abramson, R. Cox, A. Fothergill, and J. Tobin. 2018. Children and Disasters. In *Handbook of Disaster Research*, ed. H. Rodriguez, W. Donner, and J.E. Trainor, 2nd ed., 243–262. New York: Springer.

Phillips, B.D., D.S.K. Thomas, A. Fothergill, and L. Blinn-Pike, eds. 2009. *Social Vulnerability to Disasters*. Boca Raton: CRC Press.

Pipa, T. 2006. Weathering the Storm: The Role of Local Nonprofits in the Hurricane Katrina Relief Effort. *Nonprofit Sector Research Fund*. Aspen Institute.

Reeves, A. 2011. Political Disaster: Unilateral Powers, Electoral Incentives, and Presidential Disaster Declarations. *The Journal of Politics* 73 (4): 1142–1151.

Salkowe, R.S., and J. Chakraborty. 2009. Federal Disaster Relief in the U.S.: The Role of Political Partisanship and Preference in Presidential Disaster Declarations and Turndowns. *Journal of Homeland Security and Emergency Management* 6 (1): article 28.

Schmidtlein, M.C., C. Finch, and S.L. Cutter. 2008. Disaster Declarations and Major Hazard Occurrences in the United States. *The Professional Geographer* 60 (1): 1–14.

Shaw, R., and K. Goda. 2004. From Disaster to Sustainable Civil Society: The Kobe Experience. *Disasters* 28 (1): 16–40.

Sobel, R.S., and P.T. Leeson. 2006. Government's Response to Hurricane Katrina: A Public Choice Analysis. *Public Choice* 127 (1–2): 55–73.

———. 2007. The Use of Knowledge in Natural-Disaster Relief Management. *The Independent Review* 11 (4): 519–532.

Springer, C.G. 2009. Emergency Managers as Change Agents. *Ideas from an Emerging Field: Teaching Emergency Management in Higher Education* 12 (1): 197–211.

Storr, V.H., and S. Haeffele-Balch. 2012. Post-Disaster Community Recovery in Heterogeneous, Loosely Connected Communities. *Review of Social Economy* 70 (3): 295–314.

Storr, V.H., S. Haeffele-Balch, and L.E. Grube. 2015. *Community Revival in the Wake of Disaster: Lessons in Local Entrepreneurship*. New York: Palgrave Macmillan.

Thaler, R., and C. Sunstein. 2008. *Nudge: Improving Decisions About Health, Wealth and Happiness*. New York: Penguin Press.

Thomas, D.S.K., B.D. Phillips, W.E. Lovekamp, and A. Fothergill, eds. 2013. *Social Vulnerability to Disasters*. 2nd ed. Boca Raton: CRC Press.

Tierney, K.J. 2007. Testimony on Needed Emergency Management Reforms. *Journal of Homeland Security and Emergency Management* 4 (3): 15.

Veenema, T.G., ed. 2018. *Disaster Nursing and Emergency Preparedness for Chemical, Biological, and Radiological Terrorism and Other Hazards*. 4th ed. New York: Springer.

Wisner, B., P. Blaikie, T. Cannon, and I. Davis. 2004. *At Risk: Natural Hazards, People's Vulnerability, and Disasters*. 2nd ed. New York: Routledge.

2

The Rules of the Game and Post-Disaster Rebuilding and Recovery

Laura E. Grube

2.1 Introduction

In the context of the United States, federal government plays a large role in post-disaster response and rebuilding. The Federal Emergency Management Agency (FEMA) establishes the framework and systems for disaster response, including the National Incident Management System (NIMS), which describes (1) resource management before, during, and after a disaster; (2) coordination; and (3) communications and information management.[1] Federal government has considerable resources available for disaster assistance. FEMA's Disaster Relief Fund (DRF) budget for 2020 was approximately 48 billion, with 18 billion enacted for 2020 and $30 billion carrying over from the previous year. These figures do no include emergency appropriations. These additional appropriations can range from hundreds of millions a year to (in the year of Hurricane Katrina) $50.4 billion (de Rugy n.d.). FEMA can also leverage assistance from other departments and agencies, for example, the National Guard

L. E. Grube (✉)
Department of Economics, Beloit College, Beloit, WI, USA
e-mail: grubel@beloit.edu

© The Author(s) 2020
S. Haeffele, V. H. Storr (eds.), *Government Responses to Crisis*, Mercatus Studies in Political and Social Economy, https://doi.org/10.1007/978-3-030-39309-0_2

(approved through a state governor) or military (through the secretary of the Department of Defense) (FEMA 2013). FEMA has access to considerable human capital; FEMA has thousands of employees trained to deal with crisis situations, and contracts with many more.

Unsurprisingly then, there is a substantial literature on government efforts following a disaster. The literature represents a variety of perspectives, including the views of emergency management professionals and social scientists. Perry and Lindell (2003), writing in the aftermath of September 11, provide ten guidelines for preparedness, emphasizing the importance of accurate knowledge, inter-organizational coordination, and training, in addition to planning. Buck et al. (2006) analyze the effectiveness of the Incident Command System (ICS) across nine disasters and point to a few key findings, including that such systems work best when those who are utilizing them are part of a community. Jensen and Thompson (2016) describe the literature on the potential benefits of ICS such as standardization and a system that is flexible, scalable, and applicable to a wide range of crises. Notably, there is also literature that is more skeptical of government preparedness and response efforts. Referring to ICS, Waugh (2009, 172) states: "such systems, by their very nature, are inflexible, slow, and cumbersome and would be much less adaptable in task environments characterized by uncertainty and rapid change."

The literature has been largely silent, however, on the role that government plays related to "the rules of the game." The rules of the game—for example, that private property will be protected—shape incentives and, in turn, direct individuals toward or away from certain activities. The rules of the game serve this function during mundane times and in the aftermath of disaster. During mundane times, the rules of the game are known and even taken for granted, incorporated into everyday decisions. This may include, for example, rules around what speed is permissible on certain roads. The speed limit facilitates individuals getting to their destinations and promotes social coordination. In the post-disaster context, these rules include when people are allowed to return to their neighborhoods, who is eligible for assistance and how to obtain assistance, and what (re)building requirements exist. These rules are especially important because they bring some predictability in a highly uncertain environment. If the rules are clear and known in advance, they can also contribute to a quicker recovery.

In this chapter, I focus on the role of government related to the rules of the game, specifically, how government can (1) help to ensure that rules are clear and known in advance, (2) protect private property rules, and (3) support rules that allow local actors to step in. Admittedly, by focusing on the rules of the game, I also shift my attention to rebuilding and recovery, and de-emphasis initial response. Next, I elaborate on the importance of rules and why these three particular rules are critical in the post-disaster environment. Then, I discuss how these rules play out, drawing on examples from the literature.

2.2   The Importance of Clear Rules

In the weeks and months following a disaster, there is extreme uncertainty. Residents want to know if the job that they had before the storm still be available after the storm and, if so, when they will be able to return to work. What businesses will decide to rebuild? Business owners are eager to know whether customers will return. Other aspects of community life may weigh heavily on people's minds. Will the local schools be of the same quality after the storm? How will churches be affected? What congregants will return, and what church programs will continue after the storm? Scholars have written on how this scenario presents a collective action problem. The costs of rebuilding are high and include cleanup activities as well as hiring contractors to demolish damaged property and put up new drywall, repair electrical, and install new appliances. The benefits are unknown and depend on the actions of others. Faced with costs and unclear benefits, many people adopt a "wait and see" strategy. Local actors play a key role in (1) increasing the benefits of return and (2) increasing the probability that individuals return and rebuild (Chamlee-Wright and Storr 2009a; Storr et al. 2015).

Governments can help to ensure that there is not an impasse. The literature in political economy and constitutional political economy emphasizes that general rules are essential for individual decision making. Hayek (2007, 112) explains,

[The Rule of Law] means that government in all its actions is bound by rules fixed and announced beforehand—rules which make it possible to foresee with fair certainty how the authority will use its coercive powers in given circumstances and to plan one's individual affairs on the basis of this knowledge.

Clear rules are important because they (1) help individuals to determine the relative payoffs of action and (2) contribute to greater predictability (Hayek 1973; Brennan and Buchanan 2000). When individuals are confronted with so many moving parts—cleaning up mud and debris, preparing meals without electricity, finding a new day-care arrangement—government can maintain some level of predictability by offering clear rules that are known in advance.

It is worth noting that delays in the rebuilding process post disaster can be especially devastating. The longer buildings go without repairs, the more likely it is that buildings will deteriorate (e.g. a roof in need of repair can impact the integrity of an entire building as wind and water penetrate interior walls and floors). Further, if individuals are delayed in rebuilding, others who are considering whether to return will be less likely to do so if they perceive that the process will be more difficult than anticipated, or if they do not believe that others are rebuilding (and thus, face the risk of rebuilding and not having neighbors return). And, the longer that people stay in another place (e.g. the place they have evacuated to), the more likely they are to permanently stay because they may have enrolled children in school, have found an apartment or home, and may also have found employment. These are then known realities, while going back to the affected area presents an unknown.

In the aftermath of disasters, government has a role to play in (1) ensuring that people know the rules of the game, (2) protecting private property rights, and (3) allowing local actors to step in. Government can ensure that, for example, residents and business owners know when they will be allowed back to their properties, what the requirements are for rebuilding, and what assistance is available, as well as who qualifies and how to apply. When these rules are clear and known in advance, people understand what steps they need to take to begin rebuilding, and they can prioritize and plan when they will do various tasks. For example, if a building permit is required, but the process is straightforward (and relatively fast), a business owner can start to rebuild quickly. If rebuilding rules are similarly clear, then she has less risk of needing to start over and redo work that she had already completed.

By protecting private property, governments also encourage rebuilding and recovery. If residents feel uncertain about their property rights, they will be less likely to rebuild or make investments to their property. This uncertainty can lead to a "wait and see" strategy that is detrimental to recovery. Recall that the longer that residents wait to return and rebuild, the worse the damage may become to their homes and the more likely it is that they will relocate (Chamlee-Wright and Storr 2009b). Experience in the aftermath of Hurricane Katrina (2005) and the tornado in Tuscaloosa, Alabama (2011), shows that efforts to centrally plan recovery with large city redevelopment programs may actually retard recovery if residents and business owners feel uncertain in their property rights (Beito and Smith 2012; Chamlee-Wright 2007, 2010).

Relatedly, state and local governments can adopt rules that allow local actors to respond and begin rebuilding activities more quickly. For example, local governments can minimize the period when residents are not allowed back into their homes because of safety concerns, acknowledging that delays are similarly costly to recovery. Additionally, state and local governments can take steps to reduce the costs of rebuilding, such as relaxing occupational licensing rules (or at a minimum, allowing tradespeople who are licensed in other states to do work). Licensing rules seek to address asymmetric information problems in which consumers do not know about the quality of the tradespeople offering services. Licensing rules also limit the supply of tradespeople, which, in the post-disaster context, leads to slower rebuilding and recovery. Skarbek (2008) notes that Florida, a state that is frequently hit by hurricanes, has eased licensing restrictions for roofers and did not experience a noticeable increase in complaints about inadequate workmanship. Lastly, local governments may consider easing the process for obtaining building permits, again, to facilitate rebuilding and recovery.

Below, I provide evidence that further elaborates on these three roles that government can play following disaster. I rely on interviews conducted in the aftermath of Hurricane Katrina (2005); the tornadoes in

Joplin, Missouri, and Tuscaloosa, Alabama (2011); and Hurricane Sandy (2012). These interviews were conducted by Mercatus Center researchers.[2]

2.3 Government and the Rules of the Game After Disaster

2.3.1 The Importance of Clear Rules That Are Known in Advance

In the post-disaster context, individuals are navigating relatively uncharted territory. Residents will likely confront challenges that they do not have experience with, such as obtaining a building permit to repair or replace a damaged home, or applying for FEMA assistance. If residents do not understand the process for obtaining a building permit or are unsure about what assistance they may receive to help pay for their damaged home, things may remain at a standstill. Delays present further risk to rebuilding and long-term recovery.

Government (and in this case, local governments) can aid in the rebuilding and recovery process by ensuring that rules are widely known and known in advance and by making rules, whenever possible, less complicated.

Hurricane Katrina devastated the Gulf Coast and brought significant flooding to New Orleans, Louisiana. Parts of the city experienced flood levels above 12 feet. Rebuilding would mean repairing the city's elaborate levee system and understanding future risk of flooding in the various communities across the city. Unfortunately, a series of missteps only aggravated rebuilding efforts (Chamlee-Wright 2007). In April 2006, FEMA released guidelines for how high buildings would need to be elevated to protect against future water. These rules, however, were not adopted into local building codes (leaving an inconsistency in rules for residents). To make matters worse, it was then determined that the guidelines were based on outdated flood maps. The new, updated flood maps were scheduled to be released a year later (NPR 2016).

These rules then were not helpful for homeowners trying to understand what they needed to do to be able to rebuild (i.e. what elevation they needed to achieve) or what their risk was of future flooding. In this context, it is easy to understand why residents did not rebuild. If residents heard about elevation requirements and then heard that they were based on faulty information, they will be understandably cautious about how they rebuild and may wait until there is further clarity (which, again, can have an impact on how many people return and rebuild).

In addition, clarity around rules is important when assistance is offered. If an event is declared a disaster by the president, then individuals impacted by the disaster may be eligible for disaster assistance. Residents with damaged or destroyed homes may apply for assistance through the Individuals and Households Program (IHP). Following a disaster, individuals must get rid of debris, obtain cleaning supplies, and sort through household items, while also determining how they will feed themselves and their families, locating a temporary place to live, and finding day care or assistance for elderly family. The need to commit additional thinking to tasks that we take for granted during mundane times causes stress and inevitably makes it even more difficult to focus on paperwork, such as applications for assistance.

Grube et al. (2018) investigate IHP assistance to residents in the wake of Hurricane Sandy in 2012. Specifically, the authors ask if there are factors aside from damage that influence who receives federal disaster assistance. Grube et al. (2018) find that having at least a high school–level education results in more assistance, and that being foreign born has the opposite impact. The findings suggest that complexities in the process of applying for post-disaster federal aid do impact the ability (of some) to receive aid. The authors note, "Those with at least a high school degree are more likely to be employed in jobs that require employees to frequently read through paperwork, fill out forms, and file documents" (Grube et al. 2018, 589). Other scholars, including Morrow (1997) and Fothergill et al. (1999), have noted that the ability to fill out forms and "deal with bureaucracies" is important for navigating the assistance process.

In both of these examples, not knowing the rules in advance and relying on a complicated set of rules made it more difficult for communities to rebuild and recover.

2.3.2   Protecting Private Property

Bad rules—for example, building codes that rely on outdated flood maps—put private property at risk. In the aftermath of disaster, other policies, including labeling certain communities as future green space or planning to redevelop entire square blocks, introduce more uncertainty and slow rebuilding and recovery. Policies and actions by local officials should respect and protect property rights.

In April 2011, an EF4 tornado tore through Tuscaloosa, Alabama. Approximately 1500 people were injured and, tragically, 65 were killed.[3] Over 7000 buildings were damaged or destroyed. One month later, in May 2011, an EF5 tornado devastated Joplin, Missouri. The tornado caused over 1000 injuries and 158 deaths, making it the deadliest tornado in the United States since 1947.[4] The path of the tornado, three-quarters of a mile in width, damaged or destroyed over 7500 housing units and 550 businesses.[5]

As the two communities began to take stock of the damage and consider rebuilding and recovery, they decided on two very different paths. Beito and Smith (2012) describe how the city council in Joplin rolled back several regulations, including some related to occupational licensing and zoning mandates. The authors quote a Joplin resident, who said,

> When you have the magnitude of that disaster, really the old ways of doing things are suspended for a while until you create whatever normal is … The government was realistic to know that there is a period of time when common sense, codes and laws that are in place to protect people are suspended for the sake of the greater good. (Beito and Smith 2012, n.p.)

Such policies allowed Joplin to rebound quickly. In fact, schools were able to open on time for the 2011–2012 school year, less than 90 days after the tornado devastated the town (Smith and Sutter 2017).

Tuscaloosa took a different approach. The city decided to use the disaster as an opportunity to start over from scratch, and in the words of Tuscaloosa Mayor, Walt Maddox, "comprehensively plan and rebuild our great city better than even before" (quoted in Beito and Smith 2012). There was a 90-day construction moratorium in the disaster area while city officials drafted a master plan. For business owners, each day that they stood waiting was a day that they did not serve customers and did not collect revenues. Rather than wait it out, some relocated to a shopping center further from the city center.

The experiences in Joplin and Tuscaloosa illustrate the importance of protecting private property and allowing people back to rebuild.

2.3.3 Allowing Local Actors to Step In

In the weeks following a disaster, access may continue to be restricted for safety concerns and cleanup. After Hurricane Katrina, floodwaters remained in residential neighborhoods and had to be pumped out. Residents were not allowed to return for fear that people may become stranded and require rescue, or be exposed to toxins that had mixed into the water as it passed through oil refineries. When homes are destroyed by a tornado, an earthquake, or powerful waves, debris is scattered indiscriminately, and local city officials may restrict access to communities in order to prioritize debris removal from roads. Once roads are cleared, trucks can come through to restore power, emergency vehicles can enter in the case of further emergency, and contractors and tradespeople can begin the rebuilding process.

In addition to allowing residents to return, government can help to encourage rebuilding and recovery by allowing social and commercial entrepreneurs to do their work. Local governments can relax occupational licensing rules (at a minimum, allowing tradespeople who are licensed in other states to do work) and ease the process for obtaining building permits.

In the aftermath of Hurricane Katrina, scholars documented numerous examples of entrepreneurs who were slowed by regulations. Alice Craft-Kerney, a registered nurse and health-care provider in New Orleans, was inspired to open a health clinic in the Lower Ninth Ward after Hurricane Katrina (Storr et al. 2015). The disaster had highlighted the need for health-care services, and Craft-Kerney had grown up in the Lower Ninth Ward and felt an obligation to help those in the community. Craft-Kerney brought others on board with her vision and received many donations, including support from Common Ground, Home Depot, and Leaders Creating Change Through Contribution. On the day of the grand opening, however, her project was stalled. The city shut down the operation because she did not have the correct permit. After all of her hard work, she was deflated. Craft-Kerney was able to get the correct permit and opened the clinic on February 27, 2007. Delays to non-profits and businesses, however, come at a cost, which, in the aftermath of disaster, may be too high for residents to bear.

Northwest of the Lower Ninth Ward, St. Bernard Parish experienced over ten feet of flooding in some areas. Residents who returned and were eager to rebuild had to repair damaged homes and replace furniture and appliances. Mary Ann Patrick ran a furniture and appliance store before Hurricane Katrina, and in the aftermath, she was committed to rebuilding and recovery. More than a few obstacles stood in her way. First, she had to clean out 12 inches of mud that had swept into her showroom as the water came in. After cleaning the store, she applied for permits to start construction. The city, she explains, "they wouldn't give me a permit to get my phones and the electricity and that on. They kept telling me the building had to have more things done to it and stuff like this" (quoted in Storr et al. 2015, 71). She also found out that the parish planned to demolish her building and thus she had to enlist the support of her insurance company and a structural engineer to fight it. Patrick did reopen, but, again, was delayed in reopening, had to incur the costs of hiring experts to fight the parish, and therefore, customers were not able to get important furniture and appliances into their homes.

Following Hurricane Katrina, regulations around rebuilding contributed to delays in recovery.

2.4   Conclusion

The post-disaster environment is uncertain. Residents must find a temporary place to stay and must take stock of the losses. They do not know who will return and rebuild, or what their community will look like in one year or five years. The process of cleaning up, locating contractors, and also helping family members and friends can be overwhelming.

Government can provide assistance to residents to help them get back on their feet. Perhaps even more importantly, government can support the rules of the game that lead to rebuilding and recovery. Government can (1) ensure that rules are clear and known in advance, (2) protect private property, and (3) allow local actors (including entrepreneurs) to step in as soon as possible.

Admittedly, another important part of the post-disaster decision-making process is the *expectations* of government response. An individual's belief about the government's intent and capacity in the post-disaster context will inform how they engage in rebuilding and recovery (Chamlee-Wright and Storr 2009b). This point reinforces that it is not enough to have rules that support rebuilding and recovery; as importantly, government must *follow* those rules.

Notes

1. Find out more at https://training.fema.gov/nims/.
2. For an extended discussion of methodology, see Chamlee-Wright (2010) and Storr et al. (2015).
3. Data available online at http://www.srh.noaa.gov/bmx/?n=event_042720 11tuscbirm.
4. Data available online at http://www.crh.noaa.gov/sgf/?n=event_2011 may22_summary.
5. Data available online at http://www.joplinmo.org/DocumentCenter/ View/1985.

References

Beito, D., and D. Smith. 2012. Tornado Recovery: How Joplin Is Beating Tuscaloosa. *Wall Street Journal*, April 13. https://www.wsj.com/articles/SB10 001424052702303404704577309220933715082.
Brennan, G., and J.M. Buchanan. 2000. *The Reason of Rules*. Indianapolis: Liberty Fund Inc.

Buck, D., J. Trainor, and B. Aguirre. 2006. A Critical Evaluation of the Incident Command System and NIMS. *Journal of Homeland Security and Emergency Management* 3 (3): 1–27.

Chamlee-Wright, E. 2007. The Long Road Back: Signal Noise in the Post-Katrina Context. *The Independent Review* 12 (2): 235–259.

———. 2010. *The Cultural and Political Economy of Recovery.* New York: Routledge.

Chamlee-Wright, E., and V.H. Storr. 2009a. Club Goods and Post-Disaster Community Return. *Rationality and Society* 21 (4): 429–458.

———. 2009b. Expectations of Government's Response to Disaster. *Public Choice* 144 (1–2): 253–274.

de Rugy, V. n.d. *FEMA's Emergency Supplemental Track Record.* Arlington, VA: Mercatus Center at George Mason University. https://www.mercatus.org/system/files/disaster-aid-analysis-analysis-pdf.pdf.

FEMA. 2013. *National Response Framework.* 2nd ed. Washington, DC: Federal Emergency Management Agency. https://www.fema.gov/media-library-data/20130726-1914-25045-1246/final_national_response_frame-work_20130501.pdf.

Fothergill, A., E.G.M. Maestas, and J.D. Darlington. 1999. Race, Ethnicity, and Disasters in the United States: A Review of the Literature. *Disasters* 23 (2): 156–173.

Grube, L.E., R. Fike, and V.H. Storr. 2018. Navigating Disaster: An Empirical Study of Federal Assistance Following Hurricane Sandy. *Eastern Economics Journal* 44 (4): 576–593.

Hayek, F.A. 1973. *Law, Legislation and Liberty Vol. 1 Rules and Order.* Chicago: University of Chicago Press.

———. 2007. *The Road to Serfdom.* Chicago: University of Chicago Press.

Jensen, J., and S. Thompson. 2016. The Incident Command System: A Literature Review. *Disasters* 40 (1): 158–182.

Morrow, B.H. 1997. Stretching the Bonds: The Families of Andrew. In *Hurricane Andrew: Ethnicity, Gender, and the Sociology of Disasters,* ed. W.G. Peacock, B.H. Morrow, and H. Gladwin. New York: Routledge.

NPR. 2016. New Maps Label Much of New Orleans Out of Flood Hazard Area. *NPR All Things Considered,* September 30. https://www.npr.org/2016/09/30/495794999/new-maps-label-much-of-new-orleans-out-of-flood-hazard-area.

Perry, R.W., and M.K. Lindell. 2003. Preparedness for Emergency Response: Guidelines for the Emergency Planning Process. *Disasters* 27 (4): 336–350.

Skarbek, D. 2008. Occupational Licensing and Asymmetric Information: Post-Hurricane Evidence from Florida. *Cato Journal* 28 (1): 73–82.

Smith, D., and D. Sutter. 2017. Coordination in Disaster: Nonprice Learning and the Allocation of Resources After Disaster. *The Review of Austrian Economics* 30 (4): 469–492.

Storr, V.H., S. Haeffele-Balch, and L.E. Grube. 2015. *Community Revival in the Wake of Disaster Lessons in Local Entrepreneurship*. New York: Palgrave Macmillan.

Waugh, W. 2009. Mechanisms for Collaboration in Emergency Management: ICS, NIMS, and the Problem with Command and Control. In *The Collaborative Public Manager: New Ideas for the Twenty-First Century*, ed. R. O'Leary and L. Bingham, 157–175. Washington, DC: Georgetown University Press.

3

Government as Gardener: Cultivating the Environment for Private Sector Natural Disaster Response

Steven Horwitz

3.1 Introduction

Recent research has shown the effectiveness of the private sector and the non-market institutions of civil society in responding to natural disasters, especially along the Gulf Coast in the aftermath of Hurricane Katrina in 2005 (Horwitz 2009, 2010; Chamlee-Wright 2010). Private firms such as Walmart and McDonald's, along with houses of worship and various community groups, arguably did more to relieve the immediate and long-term suffering of storm victims than did the various levels of government, especially federal agencies like the Federal Emergency Management Agency (FEMA). Given the effectiveness of these non-governmental institutions, what role is there for the various levels of government in responding to disasters?

In this chapter, I offer some answers to that question. Specifically, I will argue that governments should restrict themselves to being the clarifier

S. Horwitz (✉)
Department of Economics, Ball State University, Muncie, IN, USA
e-mail: sghorwitz@bsu.edu

© The Author(s) 2020
S. Haeffele, V. H. Storr (eds.), *Government Responses to Crisis*, Mercatus Studies in Political and Social Economy, https://doi.org/10.1007/978-3-030-39309-0_3

and enforcer of the "rules of the game." In order for the private sector and civil society to facilitate the coordination process among residents, the rules of the game need to be restricted to what F. A. Hayek (1977) called "rules of just conduct" and codified clearly and enforced evenly. In practice, this means that government responses to natural disasters should focus on "first, doing no harm" and "keeping promises." The provision of law and order and the clarification of the rules of the game are sufficient to allow other actors to move forward with recovery. In general, this will work best at the most local level possible. Governments will be most effective if they see themselves as gardeners fertilizing the soil and removing the weeds so that the private sector and civil society can grow and do what they do best. Attempting to do more than cultivating the right environment for recovery will prevent those institutions from getting the job done.

3.2 Civil Society and the Private Sector

The story of the federal government's ineffective response to Hurricane Katrina is widely known. Less well known is the story of the effective responses from both the private sector and a variety of civil society institutions. Brief summaries of both of those stories are necessary to understand the case for the particular role government can play as a facilitator of private sector and civil society relief and recovery efforts.[1]

In the immediate aftermath of Katrina's landfall near New Orleans, government at various levels and the private sector and community groups began to respond. FEMA's response to the unfolding disaster was both late and ineffective, generating a great deal of public criticism, especially after President Bush's public praise of the job done by FEMA head Michael Brown. FEMA staff did not really arrive on scene until almost ten days had passed, and even then, it was not clear how helpful their efforts were. Their attempt to help by providing temporary housing in the form of trailers for displaced residents backfired when the trailers were discovered to have unacceptably high levels of formaldehyde, which made residents sick. Numerous local government officials criticized the federal response at the time, with several of them contrasting the failures of FEMA with the way in which private sector actors, especially Walmart, were able to get much-needed goods into the damaged areas. The mayor of one New Orleans suburb observed that Walmart's quick arrival with necessities after the storm hit prevented his city from seeing any significant looting. The irony here is that the first responsibility of governments is to maintain law and order, yet not only did many levels of government fail to do so in the days following landfall, it was the quick action of the private sector that helped to prevent chaos by reducing the incentive to loot.

What exactly did the private sector and other institutions do to provide relief and recovery? The most important thing the private sector did was to make goods available in damaged areas as quickly as possible. In some cases, this meant trucking in basic supplies and giving them away to local residents. In addition, a number of firms, including major stores such as Walmart and McDonald's, worked quickly to re-open stores damaged by the storm so that they could supply the needs of those cleaning up from the storm. Walmart's response was the biggest and best known. In the roughly three weeks after the August 29 landfall, Walmart brought almost 2500 truckloads of goods into the Gulf Coast region, particularly the New Orleans area. Walmart also dispatched a number of trucks full of necessities to Houston, which had become home to many Katrina evacuees. Home Depot similarly contributed to the relief effort, shipping in 800 truckloads of supplies while also transporting 1000 of its own employees into the affected areas to oversee the distribution of those supplies. Their response was much quicker than that of the federal government, which did not arrive with supplies until days, and in some cases weeks, had passed.

Getting stores re-opened was also a key part of the private sector's contribution to the recovery process. By ten days after landfall, Walmart had re-opened all but 15 of the 126 stores that had been damaged by the storm, as well as getting two distribution centers up and running. McDonald's had a similar record of success. With over 500 restaurants closed due to either damage or power outages at one point, they were able to get 80 percent of them re-opened a week after Katrina's landfall. This pattern of effective private sector response has been seen in other disaster recovery efforts since Katrina, including the May 2016 fires in Fort

McMurray, Alberta, in Canada and Hurricane Harvey along the Texas and Louisiana Gulf Coast in August 2017. The response to Harvey included major efforts by Walmart, HEB grocery stores, and Anheuser-Busch InBev, among numerous other private sector firms.[2]

In addition to the private sector, the non-state institutions of civil society played a big role in the response to Katrina and subsequent storms. These are what Alexis de Tocqueville ([1835] 2012) called "associations": everything from houses of worship, to neighborhood and homeowner groups, to community organizations were involved in the recovery process. For example, church groups were central in providing resources and services to the Vietnamese community in New Orleans East. The Mary Queen of Vietnam Catholic Church was particularly important in enabling the community to respond, thanks both to excellent clerical leadership and to its ability to provide for "club goods" necessary for residents to return to the area (Chamlee-Wright and Storr 2009). Other research emphasizes the importance of the social capital created by a flourishing civil society, which leaves scope for acts of social entrepreneurship that can discover new opportunities for social coordination outside of the market (Chamlee-Wright and Storr 2010, 2011; Storr et al. 2015).

Even households can play crucial roles in disaster relief (Horwitz 2018). Community leaders found opportunities to put displaced residents in touch with each other as a way to overcome the "who goes first?" problem that can prevent people from returning to disaster-stricken areas. The New Orleans East neighborhood was a model for recovery, as it came back to something near normal much more quickly than many of the other hard-hit neighborhoods. Other neighborhoods in the New Orleans area that fared better after storm tended to be ones where Tocquevillian associations were strong or wide enough to enable effective community action and social coordination.

Given this, admittedly too brief, summary of the effectiveness of the private sector and civil society, what role is left for government? If markets are good at moving resources to where they need to be and the Tocquevillian voluntary associations of civil society are good at creating and deploying social capital and social entrepreneurship, governments should probably stay out of those areas. Instead, as I explore below, what government should be doing is ensuring that the "rules of the game" under which people in these other sectors act are clear and consistent and enforced fairly. Rather than trying to solve problems directly itself, government should create the conditions under which citizens can do so more effectively for themselves.

3.3   The Rules of the Game

Understanding the role of government as a rule enforcer requires that we dig a little deeper into the role that rules play in a complex society. In two papers, Hayek ([1937] 1948, [1945] 1948) offered a theory of social coordination that focused on the division of knowledge in society. In the 1937 paper, "Economics and Knowledge," he was attempting to clarify the economist's understanding of equilibrium, but in doing so, he provided a much broader way of thinking about social order (Hayek [1937] 1948). Hayek argued that if we are going to get any sort of social order, it will have to involve being able to form reasonably correct expectations of the future. The ability to both plan for the future and then have the knowledge necessary to execute those plans successfully is at the core of the emergence of social order. The challenging part of this process, Hayek argued, was that we must therefore not only form correct expectations about the objective facts of the world but also have correct expectations about the actions and expectations of other actors. For example, successfully executing my plan to build a certain number of houses may well depend on how accurately I understand the expectations of others who might wish to use some of those same resources for a different project. Economic equilibrium, and implicitly a broader conception of perfect social coordination, could be understood as a world in which all of those expectations were correct, enabling everyone's plans to be executed as intended.

As he put it in the 1945 paper, "The Use of Knowledge in Society," the fundamental problem society faces is "a problem of the utilization of knowledge which is not given to anyone in its totality" (Hayek [1945] 1948, 78). Individuals each possess knowledge that is local and contextual and often inarticulate, so how is it possible that others can access that knowledge in the ways necessary to produce economic and social coordination? How can we make the plans of others part of our own planning process when none of us can articulate all that we know that is relevant to our actions? Hayek's answer was that the price system was the way in which we were able to access the knowledge of others and learn from our mistakes, and thereby correct our expectations. It is market prices that make it possible for us to use knowledge held by others to form better expectations and thereby enhance economic and social coordination.

Hayek and others have also conceptualized the market as a form of a game played according to a particular set of rules. The rules serve to define the boundaries of the market and what sorts of behavior is acceptable within it. If the fundamental characteristic of the market is that it is an arena for exchange, then there is a clear need for a set of rules by which exchange takes place. Exchange requires ownership, so at the very least actors need to know what constitutes "ownership" and then what conditions constitute a legitimate exchange. This is why the rules governing property and contract are among the most important in ensuring that the game of exchange can proceed most effectively.

The importance of rules is that they enable people to form reliable expectations of the behavior of others. We can see this in the context of actual games. What defines something as a game is the set of rules by which people play. What makes basketball "basketball" is that there is a set of rules about how the players can behave. Knowing that a shot from beyond a certain line on the court counts for three points rather than two, or that you cannot kick the ball, is a rule that enables players (as well as coaches, general managers, and owners) to form expectations about the behavior of others. It also provides the framework for other kinds of game-related decision-making. For example, when the NBA added the three-point shot many years ago, it changed the incentives facing management with respect to what sorts of players to draft, not to mention changing the incentives facing young players about what skills to develop. All of these rules shape the way the game is played and strategies are formulated. When the rules change, the incentives facing players change, and the latter change their behavior as a result. And if the rules are not clear, players do not know what to expect from other players, making it harder to play the game successfully.[3]

The same argument applies to economic and social coordination. The rules of the social game have to be clearly known and fairly enforced. The rules about property and contract are particularly important. Property owners not only need to know what they can and cannot do with their property, they need to have sufficient assurance that their rights to that property will be protected from both private and public predation in order to make the long-term investments that economic growth, including natural disaster recovery, requires. Actors need to know what constitutes a legitimate contract, and that the terms of those contracts will be honored by the law, for many of the same reasons. Having clear rules about those activities enables reliable expectation formation.

None of this is to say that rules should not ever change. The key for forming the accurate expectations required for social coordination is that the rules are stable. They need not be permanent. Rules can and should change, but those changes should not be sudden and large in scale. They should be done with sufficient warning so as to enable actors to shift their expectations. Rules should also not change frequently, even if the changes themselves are marginal. Frequent rule changes upset the stability needed for accurate expectation formation. Consider what would happen if the NBA kept eliminating then reinstating the three-point line, or adjusting the height of the basket every few years. As games change, there will be legitimate reasons to think about changing the rules. In the context of sports, bigger, faster, and stronger players might make such changes necessary.[4] Rule changes, however, need to be made gradually and with as much advance warning as possible. The worst possible thing is to make major rule changes or to change the rules frequently. In particular, rule changes should never take place in the middle of the game. As we will see in the next section, this can be a serious problem for disaster recovery.

From this perspective, the fundamental role of government in the game of economic and social coordination is to ensure that the rules are well known, clear, fairly enforced, and sufficiently stable to promote accurate expectation formation. The dangers from uncertain and ambiguous rules should be clear from the prior discussion, and I will offer some specific examples below. However, one additional comment is in order. The other mistake that governments can make is to try to become one of the players. The standard reaction to natural disasters and other crises is to hand over broad new discretionary powers to governments and to expect them to play a big role in the recovery process. Giving governments more discretion will reduce the reliability of rules, as those discretionary powers are precisely the opposite of the predictability that social coordination requires. In addition, governments are "Big Players" in that they are largely immune from the profit-and-loss discipline of the market, enabling them to exercise power in ways that private firms cannot (Koppl 2002). When governments become players, they not only disrupt the playing of the game by having an unfair advantage but also are more likely to try to change the rules in ways that favor them. Limiting government involvement to the clarification and enforcement of rules is key to avoiding those problems.

3.4   Doing No Harm and Keeping Promises

One way of framing what government can and should do in natural disaster recovery is that governments should "first, do no harm" and also "keep their promises." Doing no harm will require that policymakers closely examine both existing disaster protocols and other rules and regulations in place to see whether they hamper the ability of the private sector and civil society to do their best. It also means that governments need to stop thinking that disaster recovery requires that they construct a detailed plan to ensure success. There is a role for government, as noted earlier, in clarifying and enforcing the rules, but beyond that, it runs the danger of actively causing harm. Like doctors, politicians and bureaucrats need to better understand what makes for a healthy patient and take an oath that says they will not intervene in ways that cause the patient harm. A better appreciation of the importance of prices and profits and losses in facilitating the accurate expectation formation that generates economic growth would go a long way toward "first, doing no harm."

The second major way governments can best help is to keep their promises. This promise-keeping comes in two forms. First, government must do its job at clarifying and enforcing the rules, and do so fairly. As I argued earlier, changing the rules of the game too often or too significantly will undermine the process of economic recovery and growth. One example of a potential problem is to create what we might call "disaster exceptions" to the normal rules of property and contract. These sorts of rule changes tend to upset legitimate expectations and also tend to no longer become exceptions but rather ways in which governments become "Big Players" on a more permanent basis. Second, if governments do intervene in more active ways and become a "Big Player," they should strive to announce what they intend to do clearly and publicly and stick to that course of action. If local governments promise a particular strategy for recovery, they should do their best to stick to that strategy. Constantly changing plans and strategies is the worst of both worlds, as it involves government not only doing things it does not do well, but also doing so inconsistently.

3.4.1 First, Do No Harm

So, what does this guidance look like in practice? A number of policies can fit under the umbrella of "first, do no harm," and we can separate those into policies related to immediate disaster response and those relevant to longer-term recovery. With respect to immediate response, there are two things government can do to stop getting in the way of those who are trying to help. First, and most important, representatives from the private sector and from non-profits and other institutions of civil society need to be at the table when local communities are setting up their disaster response protocols. One of the problems in the response to Katrina was that local officials often had no idea what to do when Walmart showed up with trucks of supplies or community groups wanted to set up relief centers. Some officials stopped Walmart from entering disaster-afflicted areas, others did not. Local disaster protocols need to take account of the roles that non-government actors might play and make sure that the rules about those roles are clear and known to all. After Katrina, Texas was a leader in this sort of integration, and that seems to have paid off in the very smooth and quick response to Hurricane Harvey.

A second area of importance in the immediate response is "Good Samaritan" laws. People who try to provide medical and other assistance during flooding or other storm-related crises need to know what the rules are that apply to such situations. Many localities have Good Samaritan laws that shield those who try to render assistance from legal action by victims, but those laws vary and are often not clear. Making those laws clearer and well known, and trying to provide the maximum protection possible would further encourage the sort of immediate assistance that disaster response requires.

To help ensure longer-term recovery, governments should focus on three areas where they can avoid doing harm by changing existing policies that prevent healthy recovery. The first such policy change is to relax or eliminate zoning, occupational licensure, and other business regulations that make it difficult to open (and re-open) new businesses, especially small ones. Not only are these kinds of regulations harmful to prosperity generally, but they are especially problematic as communities attempt to recover quickly from natural disasters. In a study of the effect of occupational licensure laws on recovery in Louisiana (which kept such laws) and Florida (which eased them), David Skarbek (2010) found that Florida recovered more quickly from hurricanes, as it was able to attract in more labor and keep wages competitive. Similarly, relaxing or eliminating restrictive zoning laws as well as business licenses and unnecessary regulations with respect to housing construction will generate a much quicker, and less expensive, recovery.[5]

Second, governments should adopt policies that encourage, or at least that do not discourage, the inflow of labor, both domestic and foreign. The reconstruction and recovery process will increase the demand for labor and thereby push up wages. Those higher wages will attract new labor from elsewhere in the country and perhaps from abroad. If that new labor is allowed to migrate to the disaster area, it will push wages back down and provide the labor needed for recovery. Policies that restrict labor mobility, including everything from occupational licensure laws to union rules to federal limits on immigration, prevent the demand for labor from being met and make recovery more expensive and slower.

Finally, governments should get out of the business of constructing recovery plans. In their study of the recovery of Joplin, Missouri, after a tornado strike in 2011, Daniel J. Smith and Daniel Sutter (2013) document the ways the city allowed the business and non-profit community to lead recovery, rather than laying out a detailed plan for them to follow.

Smith and Sutter argue that the lack of a top-down plan was an important element of Joplin's quick recovery, especially compared to other tornado-damaged cities that used the damage as an opportunity for a top-down reconstruction. They also compare Joplin's success to the longer, slower recovery in New Orleans, which also was beset by numerous, often conflicting, recovery plans. One of the best ways governments can avoid doing harm is to restrict themselves to the clarification and enforcement of the rules rather than trying to influence the outcome of the game.

3.4.2 Keep Your Promises

Part of the process of clarifying and enforcing the rules is to make sure that the rules are stable (though not fixed) and consistent. Inconsistent and constantly changing rules make it much more difficult for the private sector and civil society to formulate expectations and plans that will generate economic and social coordination. Emily Chamlee-Wright (2007, 237) has argued that these sorts of problems were important in explaining the slow recovery in New Orleans after Katrina: "public policy is distorting the signals emerging from markets and civil society that would otherwise foster a swift and sustainable recovery." She ties this specifically to Robert Higgs's (1997) concept of "regime uncertainty," which refers to the way in which constantly changing and/or uncertain rules, especially with respect to government's role in the market, discourage plan formation and long-run investment. In New Orleans, the constantly changing recovery plans, along with uncertainty generated by FEMA, made it very difficult for residents to make credible plans to return and then to know what they needed to do to rebuild once they came back. Chamlee-Wright's (2007, 255) conclusion parallels the argument of this chapter:

> The best way policymakers can avoid problems of regime uncertainty in the aftermath of a disaster is to respect and continue to enforce private property rights and the rule of law, so that individuals, communities, and commercial and civil society organizations can manage the rebuilding themselves. To the extent that the government deems it necessary to adjust rules pertinent to the rebuilding process, such adjustments must respect

the basic freedoms afforded by private property rights and the rule of law. Further, such rule changes must be made quickly, clearly, and credibly.

This is how government best creates the right environment for recovery.

Another form of promise-keeping is to not make "emergency exceptions" to long-standing rules, particularly when those exceptions move governments away from the role of rule enforcer and give them more power to dictate outcomes. The same processes that generate economic coordination during normal conditions do so during and after disasters. Laws that prevent sellers from raising prices during disasters are one sort of "emergency exception." Price controls prevent prices from doing their job in signaling the scarcity of resources and thereby attracting new supplies of the resources to the affected areas. We let prices do this job in normal times, and it is a necessary part of the process of economic growth. Emergency exceptions are not only examples of governments not keeping promises and thereby creating generalized uncertainty about the rules but can have very specific detrimental effects on recovery. Natural disasters do not change the laws of economics, nor do they change the basic insight that the most important task of governments is to clarify and enforce the rules of property and contract, and bind themselves to those same rules.

3.5   The Role of Decentralization

Even as governments abide by all of the above guidelines, they should also strive to assign responsibility for disaster recovery to the most local unit of government possible. Most federal disaster response agencies are located in places physically distant from where disasters tend to strike. FEMA is headquartered in Washington, DC, as are other federal agencies, and even if they have regional offices scattered throughout the rest of the country, they are unlikely to be as in touch with the needs of the local community as are municipal governments. The result is that most federal disaster relief agencies find it hard to respond in locally effective ways because they lack those local connections. Decentralizing responsibility, or placing responsibility in the hands of agencies that are structured in a highly decentralized way, will help to ensure that governments make the best possible use of the local knowledge, as stressed by Hayek ([1945] 1948). This means relying on municipal and state governments to develop disaster response protocols that include all of the relevant local actors.

The effective performance of the Coast Guard during Hurricane Katrina is instructive along these lines (Horwitz 2009). The Coast Guard has numerous local offices along the coastline and works closely with local residents, especially people with boats, who can be part of a rescue operation, as they were in both Katrina and, more recently, Harvey. The Coast Guard also has a much more decentralized command structure that gives a great deal of discretion to officers on the spot (e.g., the captain of a boat has authority over that boat, regardless of rank). These two factors were responsible for the Coast Guard being one of the few government agencies that did effective work during Katrina, rescuing over 22,000 people from the floodwaters with the help of local fishermen and others.[6] The one major government success story is the exception that proves the rule. I noted earlier that one key advantage of the private sector is how integrated firms are with their local communities in comparison to the federal government. Where local governments, or particular branches of the federal government, have those deep connections to communities, it is likely that they will perform relatively better than other government agencies. This suggests that disaster policy should empower the most local level of government feasible.

Virgil Henry Storr, Stefanie Haeffele-Balch, and Laura E. Grube (2015, chapter 8) argue similarly for the benefits of what they term, following the work of Vincent Ostrom, "polycentrism." By this they mean problem-solving approaches that have multiple individuals or organizations with the ability and responsibility to act, but also some way of communicating and coordinating among them to ensure that these multiple nodes are integrated into a whole. Polycentric systems also include competition among those with decentralized responsibility as a way to discover which kinds of actions (e.g., responses to disaster) work best. One advantage of this perspective is that it directs our attention to the ways that political actors can have sufficient freedom within polycentric political systems to discover new and better ways of doing things. Federalist political systems afford this opportunity, at least in theory, and enabling this sort of political entrepreneurship is another reason to want to put disaster response in the hands of local actors as often as possible.

Even as governments strive toward decentralization, it is important to keep in mind that decentralization is not a cure-all for the problems facing activist government responses to disasters. In the private sector, decentralization of ownership is one of two factors that ensure quick and effective responses. The other is that the prices and profits of the market serve as a way of coordinating the decisions made by the decentralized control over resources. As governments move to decentralize responsibility for disaster response to ever more local levels, it will be important to think about the ways in which those local responses will get coordinated across municipalities, as few natural disasters (other than perhaps tornadoes) affect a very small geographical area. Preparation for hurricanes and floods in particular does need to be decentralized, but it also needs to be coordinated. Ensuring that the rules are consistent across jurisdictions will be an important challenge for local and state policymakers.

3.6   Conclusion

One lesson from the history of natural disasters is that the private sector and the institutions of civil society are crucial for both an effective immediate response and a quick and long-lasting recovery. Government's role in this process is like a referee or umpire in a game or athletic contest: clarify and enforce the rules, but do not insert yourself in the game to try to direct the outcome. If governments enforce the rules of property and contract and constrain themselves by the rule of law, the private and nonprofit sectors will lead the recovery.

This does not mean that there is nothing for governments to do. Rule clarification and enforcement require their time and attention, and there are numerous policies on the books that could be relaxed or eliminated to ensure that governments both do no harm and keep their promises. Most important, local governments need to work closely with representatives from the private sector and civil society to construct disaster response and recovery protocols that are both broadly inclusive and clearly defined, as well as coordinated across jurisdictions. Through these sorts of efforts, governments act like gardeners in creating the fertile ground in which response and recovery can take place most effectively.

Notes

1. The following material draws on Horwitz (2009).
2. On the Alberta fires, see Horwitz (2016). On the private sector response to Hurricane Harvey, see Perry (2017).
3. One need only consider the ambiguities around what constitutes a "catch" in professional football over the last few years to see how unclear rules can undermine expectation formation and lead to wasted resources in endless attempts to clarify those rules or debate whether they have been accurately applied. Players become unsure what they can and cannot do in order to have a legitimate catch, and the game as a whole is harmed by this ambiguity.
4. The recent changes to the rules around kickoffs in the NFL would be an example of this, as the violence of kickoff collisions has worsened as players have become bigger and stronger.
5. Most of these regulations are local and can be changed as part of a more general disaster response planning process. For a further discussion of these sorts of regulations and their effect, especially on lower-income residents who will face the most challenges in recovery, see Horwitz (2015).
6. Those volunteer local fishermen and other boat owners are now known as the "Cajun Navy" and have played a very important role in water rescues in numerous hurricanes and flooding events since Katrina.

References

Chamlee-Wright, E. 2007. The Long Road Back: Signal Noise in the Post-Katrina Context. *The Independent Review* 12 (2): 235–259.

———. 2010. *The Cultural and Political Economy of Recovery: Social Learning in a Post-Disaster Environment*. New York: Routledge.

Chamlee-Wright, E., and V.H. Storr. 2009. Club Goods and Post-Disaster Community Return. *Rationality and Society 21* (4): 429–458.

———. 2010. The Role of Social Entrepreneurship in Post-Katrina Recovery. *International Journal of Innovation and Regional Development 2* (1/2): 149–164.

———. 2011. Social Capital as Collective Narratives and Post-Disaster Community Recovery. *The Sociological Review* 59 (2): 266–282.

de Tocqueville, A. [1835] 2012. *Democracy in America.* English ed. Ed. Eduardo Nolla and Trans. James T. Schleifer. Indianapolis: Liberty Fund.

Hayek, F. A. [1937] 1948. Economics and Knowledge. Reprinted in *Individualism and Economic Order,* 33–56. Chicago: University of Chicago Press.

———. [1945] 1948. The Use of Knowledge in Society. Reprinted in F. A. Hayek, *Individualism and Economic Order,* 77–91. Chicago: University of Chicago Press.

Hayek, F.A. 1977. *Law, Legislation, and Liberty Vol. II: The Mirage of Social Justice.* Chicago: University of Chicago Press.

Higgs, R. 1997. Regime Uncertainty Why the Great Depression Lasted So Long and Why Prosperity Resumed After the War. *The Independent Review* 1 (4): 561–590.

Horwitz, S. 2009. Wal-Mart to the Rescue: Private Enterprise's Response to Hurricane Katrina. *The Independent Review* 13 (4): 511–528.

———. 2010. Doing the Right Things: The Private Sector Response to Hurricane Katrina as a Case Study in the Bourgeois Virtues. In *Accepting the Invisible Hand: Market-Based Approaches to Social Economic Problems,* ed. M.D. White, 169–190. New York: Palgrave Macmillan.

———. 2015. Breaking Down the Barriers: Three Ways State and Local Governments Can Get out of the Way and Improve the Lives of the Poor. *Mercatus Research.* Arlington, VA: Mercatus Center at George Mason University. http://mercatus.org/publication/breaking-down-barriers-three-ways-state-and-local-governments-can-improve-lives-poor.

———. 2016. In Natural Disasters, Companies Operate Like Neighbors. *Wall Street Journal,* June 7. https://www.wsj.com/articles/in-natural-disasters-companies-operate-like-neighbors-1465338881.

———. 2018. *Households as Crisis Shock Absorbers.* SSRN Working Paper No. 3259507. https://papers.ssrn.com/sol3/papers.cfm?abstract_id=3259507.

Koppl, R. 2002. *Big Players and the Economic Theory of Expectations.* New York: Palgrave Macmillan.

Perry, M. 2017. Private Sector to the Rescue in Texas. *Carpe Diem,* August 29. http://www.aei.org/publication/private-sector-to-the-rescue-never-underestimate-the-power-of-the-private-sector-to-rise-up-to-face-any-challenge/.

Skarbek, D. 2010. Restricting Reconstruction: Occupational Licensing and Natural Disasters. In *The Political Economy of Hurricane Katrina and Community Rebound*, ed. E. Chamlee-Wright and V.H. Storr, 72–83. Cheltenham: Edward Elgar Publishing.

Smith, D.J., and D. Sutter. 2013. Response and Recovery After the Joplin Tornado Lessons Applied and Lessons Learned. *The Independent Review* 18 (2): 165–188.

Storr, V.H., S. Haeffele-Balch, and L.E. Grube. 2015. *Community Revival in the Wake of Disaster: Lessons in Local Entrepreneurship*. New York: Palgrave Macmillan.

4

The Role of the Local Emergency Manager in a Centralized System of Disaster Management

Amy Lepore

4.1 Introduction

To better understand the implications of centralization on US disaster management, a nationwide survey of county emergency managers was conducted (Crabill 2015). Crabill's study sought to identify issues of significance that might inform discussion about the expansive federal role in the day-to-day operations of local emergency management (EM). Through an inquiry about their actions in the federal financial relationship, a series of unintended consequences were identified. Among those consequences is the loss of independence that is experienced as a tradeoff for federal funds. How the emergency manager's actions relate to centralization and the local loss of independence is explored in this study by recounting his sentiments.

Somewhat surprisingly, survey responses of local emergency managers indicate agreement that the current disaster management framework is a

A. Lepore (✉)
Anthem Planning Inc., Middletown, DE, USA
e-mail: alepore@anthemplanning.com

© The Author(s) 2020
S. Haeffele, V. H. Storr (eds.), *Government Responses to Crisis*, Mercatus Studies in Political and Social Economy, https://doi.org/10.1007/978-3-030-39309-0_4

centrally planned function. In its current form, local EM operates as an arm of a highly involved federal government. Local personnel, though assigned to the level of government most proximal to the taxpayer, are often beholden to federal operating rules and the federal government as their primary source of funds. They do not operate as autonomous local public servants. Thus, their role as a federal emissary has implications for local government.

In order to better understand the emergency manager, centralization, and local impact, this chapter is structured as follows. Section 4.2 will establish the current centralized environment for EM and Sect. 4.3 will provide detail about emergency managers and their actions and will culminate in a few scenarios for consideration. Section 4.4 will explore potential threats to local autonomy or why local autonomy is important. Section 4.5 provides a conclusion.

4.2 Centralization of Payment for Emergency Management and Disaster Expenses

Despite the Federal Emergency Management Agency's (FEMA's) efforts to decentralize the accountability for disaster management, payment for emergency management expenses is largely nationalized. In 2017, two of the largest grants that benefit county offices—the Emergency Management Performance Grant (EMPG) and the Homeland Security Grant Program—totaled $350 million and over $1 billion, respectively (FEMA 2017a, 2017b). In the same year, the budget for disasters began at $7.3 billion and ended at $130 billion (Balonon-Rosen 2017).

Even after historic increases since the 1990s, local governments want more EM money. This is particularly valuable because funding from the federal government supplants the need to contribute local dollars. Thus, it is popular with politicians seeking to bring federal money back to their jurisdictions (Garrett and Sobel 2003; Sobel and Leeson 2006) and with the emergency managers, who do not have to ask their elected officials for more money during budget time. In fact, many local organizations are using EMPG as a primary source of funding for their programs; in 2012, locals reported that on average nearly a third of their budget used EMPG funds (IAEM 2012). After disasters, there is also an expectation for quick and plentiful federal funding. This funding has been so prolific that, as Birkland and DeYoung (2011, 486) point out, "[s]tate and local governments have become dependent on federal aid for disasters, blurring the division of labor in the federal-state-local emergency management relationship." Responsibility for natural disaster funding needs specifically is almost solely given to the federal government. As noted by Miao et al. (2016, 3):

> Our results suggest that disaster-induced increase in federal transfers outsizes the increase in state spending, which suggests that in most cases, the federal government acts as a full insurer for subnational natural disaster costs. This finding highlights the significant redistributional effects of natural disasters in the U.S. federal system.

Scholars generally concur that EM has been highly centralized at the federal level. Kincaid (1990) extends the understanding of centralization to include not only the offering of grants, but direct intervention by the federal government to preempt and expand its authority. The expansion of power is attractive to federal officials, who, as Kincaid has pointed out, distance themselves from their local constituents and then simultaneously intervene on state or local affairs. This level of opportunism is evident even in projects touted as examples of bottom-up planning. Birkland and Waterman (2008, 698) wrote that "FEMA sought to circumvent state governments and work directly with localities" during Project Impact. More recently, changes after September 11, 2001, and Hurricane Katrina have emphasized this usurping of the local policy space in favor of an increasingly powerful federal government (Derthick 2009). It is maintained by other scholars, however, that the presence of emergency managers at the local level and their active involvement in preparedness and response activities indicate that there is not centralization, or that it is not as extreme as others might suggest. In fact, many have called for even more money to be contributed by the federal government (Roberts 2007; Scavo et al. 2008). In this case parallels between the perceived federal responsibility for "education, social services and health care" are made with respect to the lack of funding for EM (Scavo et al. 2008, 95).

It is important to note that this discussion of funding encompasses both preparedness funding as well as post-disaster money, and that those two functions are quite different. However, as the individual emergency manager is the focus of this review, it is important to consider his role in the payment relationship and in increasing centralization. Specifically, with respect to the aforementioned skills he needs, we must consider if the emergency manager is prepared to interpret the intergovernmental back-and-forth and how he acts on centralization and the resultant lack of autonomy.

4.3   The Emergency Manager

4.3.1   Demographics, Education, and Skills

While there is a growing number of EM personnel across all sectors, Comfort (1985), Waugh (1994), and Choi (2004) note that county emergency managers are considered best positioned to respond during disasters and to manage local program and policy requirements. Therefore, this review compiled information about county-level personnel. Several studies have been conducted to ascertain demographic information about individuals serving as county emergency managers in order to better understand their experiences and attributes. Surveys employed during these studies varied widely but converge on several fronts. Research efforts by Cwiak et al. (2004), Weaver et al. (2014), and Crabill (2015) each found that emergency managers were largely white males who were older than their female counterparts on average. The authors also note, individually, that increasingly females were becoming a part of this field. Median ages were over 45 in each case. While many emergency managers were actively pursuing a degree when surveyed, degree attainment at the time of each study was over 70 percent. Between 2001 and 2005, more than 100 new academic programs were developed, resulting in a workforce with nearly double the undergraduate and graduate degrees when compared to the average American four years later, in 2009 (Blanchard 2004; O'Connor 2005; US Census Bureau 2009).

While education is important, it is also generally accepted that emergency managers should have excellent interpersonal skills (Waugh and Streib 2006). New trends in emergency management also indicate that the profession now favors education and certifications over practitioner EMS, fire, or police backgrounds (Blanchard 2004; Cwiak et al. 2004). However, despite changes in their skill sets, concerns about EM leadership quickly follow most major disasters. Those concerns are often cited as failures in communication or failures to act. This pair of problems acts in tandem and can cause immediate breakdown in any system and could conceivably be a tradeoff for decreasing levels of practical experience. In its comment on the Hurricane Katrina response, the US House Select Bipartisan Committee (2006, 1) elaborated on these challenges, noting that,

> We reflect on the 9/11 Commission's finding that 'the most important failure was one of imagination' ... Katrina was primarily a failure of initiative. But there is, of course, a nexus between the two. Both imagination and initiative—in other words, leadership—require good information. And a coordinated process for sharing it. And a willingness to use information—however imperfect or incomplete—to fuel action.

Failures to act, or decision-making failures, have been the subject of at least one study of emergency managers. Collins and Peerbolte (2012) conducted a study of local emergency managers from the Commonwealth of Virginia who identified a series of managerial skills that were still needed. Specifically, they found that emergency managers may not gather and use information appropriately in decision making and that they exhibited problems with interpretation of information. Responses which lacked objectivity and which were emotional in nature were also among the problematic findings.

4.3.2 Actions Related to Funding

We can begin to consider the emergency manager's actions as exemplifying his understanding of the centralization of funding. One action has been to form strong lobbies. Both the International Association of Emergency Managers (IAEM) and the National Association of Emergency

Managers (NEMA) promote a strong national system of emergency management and support funding increases whenever possible. Of the eight key measures of success listed by NEMA, each one is focused on increasing federal assistance for emergency management or disaster expenses (NEMA 2018). These measures are intended to express how well NEMA has done impacting national emergency management policy, yet the narrow path of impact is all about more money.

The IAEM has taken a similar stance; its 2018 legislative priorities are strictly about increasing or restoring funding (IAEM 2018). If either of these organizations has ever promoted the dissolution of some federal program due to inefficiency or inadequate outcomes, it was not made evident during this review of their documentation. Even the failures of Katrina, far larger and more devastating than what one well-funded government function might have managed, are blamed on too little funding for state and local EM offices. "The way to avoid these problems in the future is to invest in preparedness grant programs, such as the EMPG program, that are focused on achievement of the outcomes associated with the prepared jurisdiction" (Jensen 2011, 11).

The emergency manager takes other actions which might provide insight into his understanding of the federal-local funding relationship. Chiefly, he applies for or receives grants from the national level as a primary source of external funding. In fact, only 3 percent of respondents to Crabill's survey reflect the willingness to turn down federal funds (Crabill 2015).[1] The tradeoff for this decision is dramatic; 46 percent of emergency manager respondents report total dependence on the federal government for some combination of personnel, equipment, and training. Only 4 percent of respondents believed that their office had complete autonomy. The ability to "independently meet the needs of citizens and sufficient autonomy from the federal government as to act in the best interest of the organization and its citizens" is missing in many EM offices (Crabill 2015, 61). In the cases where dependence is acknowledged, the decision to accept funds is made in order to keep the doors open, regardless of local support for the effort. Among respondents, 56 percent reported that without EMPG funding, they could not sustain their program. We might infer from this that they believe that local officials would not see sufficient merit as to contribute local funds for sustainment. However, in order to keep the office alive, the emergency manager continues to use federal funding. As further centralization of the EM function occurs, this paradox is likely to remain. Because emergency managers recognize that there is little autonomy and still request more funding from the same avenues, the cycle of funding and dependence will likely continue.

4.3.3   Potential Scenarios

In this section, two scenarios are developed based on emergency manager responses to the Crabill 2015 survey. These scenarios express two sets of widely held sentiments about funding and the federal government's role. Scenario 1. The emergency manager, having sufficient education and experience to execute sound decision making, still feels powerless to rearrange his financial situation. He knows he cannot obtain local support for sustaining his office's operating budget so he gratefully accepts federal money. He does not view the requirements to implement federal standards as a loss of autonomy or, if he does, is willing to make the tradeoff. He believes it is his duty to prepare the populace and to lead the effort when disaster strikes, and that means maximizing a budget for people, equipment, and programs. He finds that when he makes decisions it is hard to act objectively when it seems his office's budget is always threatened. He likely shares the sentiments of these emergency managers with regard to EMPG funding:

- Without EMPG, I am concerned that we may not be able to fund our Emergency Management Program.
- Very beneficial. Without it, many aspects of the job, namely bringing folks together, would not be accomplished.
- If it were not for the EMPG funding my EM agency would not be able to function as it does today. It is a requirement by state law to have a

local EM agency but if there were not federal funding to help back it, the result would be just enough to get by the law.

- EMPG funding is essential to local EM programs. The EM program would be significantly reduced or duties reassigned to others if EMPG funding were reduced or eliminated.

Scenario 2. The emergency manager is acutely aware of the compromised position that local governments are in when they are the recipients of federal money. He, as an office of one, must take the courses, participate in the classes, and document the performance required by the federal government in exchange for funding. Often it seems like it is barely worth it, but local budget cuts loom. He has experienced the level of expectation of his elected officials when, after a snowstorm, they leaned heavily on him to obtain federal reimbursement for a few hundred thousand dollars. During those months, as he appealed to the state to consider his county in the declaration, he quietly wondered why such predictable events are not planned for in the local budget. He worries, along with his colleagues below, about the beliefs among his bosses that federal funding is always the answer. He likely shares the sentiments of these emergency managers with regarding to EMPG funding:

> While most think it's nice to receive federal grant dollars, the negative impact from that is our local officials in control of our agency's budget now view these dollars as an 'entitlement' and expect to receive these funds every year. This has obscured the true cost of our local EM program from these officials. If the EMPG is ever discontinued or cut back at the Federal or State level, I'm not confident the funding necessary to sustain our program at its current level would be provided by our officials.

> [The effect of EMPG is] negative in the sense that the grant has resulted on more dependence [and direction] from the federal level. Not good business to depend upon grants to conduct essential day to day business.

4.4 Threats to Local Autonomy and Analysis of the Scenarios

Scholars and courts alike have upheld the importance of local autonomy (Sullivan 2003; New York v. United States 1992; People ex rel. Le Roy v. Hurlbut 1871). In a particularly eloquent defense of local government, Justice Cooley (People ex rel. Le Roy v. Hurlbut 1871, n.p.) wrote:

> [T]he constitution has been adopted in view of a system of local government, well understood and tolerably uniform in character, existing from the very earliest settlement of the country, never for a moment suspended or displaced, and the continued existence of which is assumed; and, second, that the liberties of the people have generally been supposed to spring from, and be dependent upon that system.

While it is not in the purview necessarily of emergency managers to spend time each day with the constitution, it is appropriate for them to consider the implications of decreased autonomy. In addition to concerns about dependence is the scope creep of an increasingly powerful federal government. Even emergency management's foundational documents contain indications of increasing federal involvement and usurping of local power. A quick glance through the Stafford Act (1988, amended in 2016) gives rise to the permissions granted to bypass local and state governments. It reads that the President may

> provide accelerated Federal assistance and Federal support where necessary to save lives, prevent human suffering, or mitigate severe damage, which may be provided *in the absence of a specific request* and in which case the President—
>
> (A) shall, to the fullest extent practicable, promptly notify and coordinate with officials in a State in which such assistance or support is provided; and
> (B) *shall not, in notifying and coordinating with a State under subparagraph (A), delay or impede the rapid deployment, use, and distribution of critical resources to victims of a major disaster.* (FEMA 2016, 26–27; emphasis added)

The predicament of many emergency managers is that they have become unable to sustain their local operations without the federal government. This in turn empowers federal involvement and results in clauses like the one above, with little chance that locals or lobbyists will push back.

Other concerns also exist, given that the emergency manager operates locally but is primarily beholden to another level of government. Niskanen (1968) posed that bureaucrats may not always act in the best interest of the population they serve and might instead seek to benefit themselves. How would we know selfish actions if we saw them? Niskanen (1968) relays that, regardless of intent, it is the desire of bureaucrats to maximize financial resources, noting that even altruistic bureaucrats maximize budgets. This is evident in Scenario 1, where the emergency manager believes that in order to carry out his duties of preparing the populace for disaster, he must seek out funding wherever it can be found. Thus, picking out emergency managers who are acting in their own self-interest would be difficult, and the mindset of a singular emergency manager who believes he has this duty is not within the scope of this chapter. However, we can look to see if emergency managers "engage in considerable promotion … to augment the demand for its output" (Niskanen 1968, 303). It is difficult to "sell" preparedness activity when disasters seem unlikely. It is certainly true that emergency managers promote their bureaus, but meet resistance when there is not the threat of a disaster. Preparedness campaigns launched at the beginning of hurricane season or prior to winter serve to remind people of the risk that still seem far removed. Such campaigns might be gone were it not for FEMA, which uses grants to assist by freeing up local dollars that would have likely been spent on salaries (Crabill 2015). Still, local promotion does not seem to be nearly as effective as persuading the federal government (through the lobbying arm) to further consolidate responsibility, another activity we have been warned about by Niskanen (1968).

It is quite clear that if emergency managers are undertaking the aforementioned methods, budget maximizing and bureau promotion may contribute to their decreasing autonomy and power consolidation at the federal level. In fact, one emergency manager believed that without federal funding even the smallest of community-based efforts including "bringing folks together" was not possible (see Scenario 1 in

Sect. 4.3.3). The inability to hold a local meeting without federal intervention, if it were true, would have far-reaching effects. The emergency manager in Scenario 2 might believe instead that it is the presence of federal funding which has blinded local officials to what can and should be done locally. He laments that the actual costs of emergency management are obscured, and that the benefits of locally driven efforts are negated.

How can we best understand the position that the local emergency managers are in with respect to the federal funding relationship? What causes complacency in the face of lost autonomy? An evaluation of the principal-agency model may illuminate. The much-debated origin of the principal-agency theory rests either with Ross (1973) and Mitnick (1975) or with Jensen and Meckling (1976). For our purposes, we will borrow from Mitnick (1975, 8): "We will say that a relation of agency exists when one party, the 'agent' is acting for another party, the 'principal.'" In the case of the local-federal relationship, the local agent acts upon the direction of the federal government, or principal. As mentioned in Sects. 4.2 and 4.3, local emergency managers are often funded by and must meet goals dictated by the federal government. This arrangement is in keeping with the principal-agent theory. Mitnick (1975, 8) writes,

Agency behavior includes, generally, performing acts beneficial to a given goal of the principal; acting as representative of the principal in a matter which interests or concerns him, or otherwise affects him in some way; acting as trustee for the principal, perhaps administering something valued in the principal's interest or deciding for the principal in his interest; acting as employee of the principal, perhaps taking orders from the principal and enabling the principal to perform a task he could not perform alone; acting as substitute for the principal, where the principal is unable to act for himself in his own interest.

Thus, despite acknowledgment of the importance of local autonomy and visible signs of large-scale federal encroachment, local emergency managers are instrumental in furthering centralization.

4.5   Conclusion

Lovell (1981, 201) wrote that "the healthy local government must have the capacity to respond to local problems and to meet the diverse needs of its individual citizens." She observed that reliance on federal funding by local governments—regardless of their relative financial health—breeds financial dependence and reduces the autonomy required to make local issues a priority. Indeed, Lovell's concerns about dependence and autonomy reemerge as considerable challenges for the emergency manager.

The intention of this review was to better understand the role of the emergency manager in a system which has undergone centralization and that is caught in a cycle of dependence and lost autonomy. In order to establish a starting point, it was argued that the federal government acts as primary payer for emergency management and disaster expenses as a result of a concerted effort to centralize authority. Next, a summary of demographic, education, and skill sets was offered. When considered against available skills and actions taken by emergency managers which contribute to lost autonomy, two scenarios emerge. In the first, no consideration is given to the implications of federal control, and the emergency manager takes actions to fund as much of his budget as possible with federal dollars. Local budget situations are dire enough to obscure any concern the emergency manager might have had about centralization or why local power matters. In the second, the emergency manager is acutely aware of the implications of his actions and the actions of his local officials but feels as though he has no opportunity to make a decision that would result in dependence. Neither emergency manager actively seeks to give control to the federal government, but both are subject to the inherent want to see those roles sustained. Sustaining their roles often means taking actions to persuade the federal government to keep the money coming, permitting a consolidation of power at the national level, with implications that must be considered.

Note

1. An electronic survey was sent to 2339 county emergency managers during the fall of 2013, with 598 respondents.

References

Balonon-Rosen, P. 2017. The Business of Disaster: How Does the U.S. Spend Relief Money? *Marketplace*, November 27. http://www.marketplace.org/2017/11/27/world/business-disaster-how-does-us-spend-relief-money.

Birkland, T.A., and S.E. DeYoung. 2011. Emergency Response, Doctrinal Confusion, and Federalism in the Deepwater Horizon Oil Spill. *Publius: The Journal of Federalism* 41 (3): 471–493.

Birkland, T., and S. Waterman. 2008. Is Federalism the Reason for Policy Failure in Hurricane Katrina? *Publius: The Journal of Federalism* 38 (4): 692–714.

Blanchard, W. 2004. *Federal Emergency Management Agency (FEMA) Higher Education Project Update, December 3, 2004.* Washington, DC: Federal Emergency Management Agency. http://www.training.fema.gov/emiweb/downloads/highedbrief_course2.ppt.

Choi, S.O. 2004. Emergency Management Growth in the State of Florida. *State & Local Government Review* 36 (3): 212–226.

Collins, M.L., and S.L. Peerbolte. 2012. Public Administration Emergency Management Pedagogy: Cultivating the Habit of Critical Thinking. *Journal of Public Affairs Education* 18 (2): 315–326.

Comfort, L. 1985. Integrating Organizational Action in Emergency Management; Strategies for Change. *Public Administration Review* 45 (Special Issue: Emergency Management: A Challenge for Public Administration): 155–164.

Crabill, A. L. 2015. *The Effects of Federal Financial Assistance: Attitudes and Actions of Local Emergency Managers.* University of Delaware Thesis. http://udspace.udel.edu/handle/19716/17054.

Cwiak, C., K. Cline, and T. Karlgaard. 2004. *Emergency Management Demographics: What Can We Learn from a Comparative Analysis of IAEM Respondents and Rural Emergency Managers?* Washington, DC: Federal Emergency Management Agency. https://training.fema.gov/hiedu/surveys.aspx.

Derthick, M. 2009. The Transformation That Fell Short: Bush, Federalism, and Emergency Management. Paper for the Nelson A. Rockefeller Institute of Government, Albany, N.Y. https://rockinst.org/wp-content/uploads/2017/11/2009-08-Transformation_That_Fell-min.pdf

FEMA. 2016. *Robert T. Stafford Disaster Relief and Emergency Assistance Act, as Amended, and Related Authorities as of August 2016, Public Law 93-288.* Washington, DC: Federal Emergency Management Agency and US Congress. https://www.fema.gov/media-library/assets/documents/15271.

FEMA. 2017a. *Emergency Management Performance Grant Program.* Washington, DC: Federal Emergency Management Agency and US Congress. https://www.fema.gov/emergency-management-performance-grant-program.

FEMA. 2017b. *Homeland Security Grant Program.* Washington, DC: Federal Emergency Management Agency and US Congress. https://www.fema.gov/homeland-security-grant-program.

Garrett, T.A., and R.S. Sobel. 2003. The Political Economy of FEMA Disaster Payments. *Economic Inquiry* 41 (3): 496–509.

IAEM. 2012. *Emergency Management Performance Grant Funds: Returns on Investment at the Local Level.* Falls Church, VA: US Council of International Association of Emergency Managers. http://www.iaem.com/documents/IAEM.EMPG.ROI.Survey.Report3.5.12.pdf.

IAEM. 2018. *IAEM-USA Legislative Priorities.* Falls Church, VA: US Council of International Association of Emergency Managers. http://www.iaem.com/documents/IAEM-Legislative-Priorities-Summer2018.pdf.

Jensen, J. 2011. *Preparedness: A Principled Approach to Return on Investment.* Falls Church, VA: International Association of Emergency Managers. https://www.ndsu.edu/fileadmin/emgt/IAEM_preparedness_principled_approach_81111.pdf.

Jensen, C., and H. Meckling. 1976. Theory of the Firm: Managerial Behavior, Agency Costs and Ownership Structure. *Journal of Financial Economics* 3 (4): 305–360.

Kincaid, J. 1990. From Cooperative to Coercive Federalism. *Annals of the American Academy of Political and Social Science* 509 (1): 139–152.

Lovell, C.H. 1981. Evolving Local Government Dependency. *Public Administration Review* 41 (Special Issue: The Impact of Resource Scarcity on Urban Public Finance): 189–202.

Miao, Q., Y. Hou, and M. Abrigo. 2016. Measuring the Financial Shocks of Natural Disasters: A Panel Study of U.S. States. *National Tax Journal* 71 (1): 11–44.

Mitnick, B. M. 1975. *The Theory of Agency: A Framework.* SSR Working Paper No. ID 1021642. https://papers.ssrn.com/abstract=1021642.

National Emergency Management Association. 2018. NEMA's Role in Washington. https://www.nemaweb.org/index.php/about/government-relations. Accessed December 15, 2017.

New York v. United States. 1992. *US Supreme Court, Volume 505, U.S. 144.* https://supreme.justia.com/cases/federal/us/505/144/case.html.

Niskanen, W.A. 1968. The Peculiar Economics of Bureaucracy. *The American Economic Review* 58 (2): 293–305.

O'Connor, M. J. 2005. *From Chaos to Clarity: Educating Emergency Managers.* University of Akron Dissertation. https://etd.ohiolink.edu/!etd.send_file?acc ession=akron1123250948&disposition=inline.

People ex rel. Le Roy v. Hurlbut. 1871. *Michigan Supreme Court.* https://www. ravellaw.com/opinions/35a38466d5974971fa5620128e4c98be.

Roberts, P.S. 2007. Dispersed Federalism as a New Regional Governance for Homeland Security. *Publius: The Journal of Federalism* 38 (3): 416–443.

Ross, S. 1973. The Economic Theory of Agency: The Principal's Problem. *The American Economic Review* 63 (2): 134–139.

Scavo, C., R.C. Kearney, and R.J. Kilroy. 2008. Challenges to Federalism: Homeland Security and Disaster Response. *Publius: The Journal of Federalism* 38 (1): 81–110.

Sobel, R.S., and P.T. Leeson. 2006. Government's Response to Hurricane Katrina: A Public Choice Analysis. *Public Choice* 127: 55–73.

Sullivan, J. 2003. The Tenth Amendment and Local Government. *The Yale Law Journal* 112 (7): 1935–1942.

US Census Bureau. 2009. *American FactFinder – Results.* Washington, DC: US Census Bureau. https://factfinder.census.gov/faces/tableservices/jsf/pages/ productview.xhtml?pid=ACS_16_5YR_S1501&prodType=table.

US House Select Bipartisan Committee to Investigate the Preparation for and Response to Hurricane Katrina. 2006. *A Failure of Initiative: The Final Report of the Select Bipartisan Committee to Investigate the Preparation for and Response to Hurricane Katrina, H. Rept. 109-377.* Washington, DC: US House of Representatives. https://katrina.house.gov/.

Waugh, W.L. 1994. Regionalizing Emergency Management: Counties as State and Local Government. *Public Administration Review* 54 (3): 253–258.

Waugh, W.L., and G. Streib. 2006. Collaboration and Leadership for Effective Emergency Management. *Public Administration Review* 66 (s1): 131–140.

Weaver, J., L.C. Harkabus, J. Braun, S. Miller, R. Cox, J. Griffith, and R.J. Mazur. 2014. An Overview of a Demographic Study of United States Emergency Managers. *Bulletin of the American Meteorological Society* 95 (2): 199–203.

5

Recognizing Vulnerability and Capacity: Federal Initiatives Focused on Children and Youth Across the Disaster Lifecycle

Lori Peek and Simone Domingue

5.1 Prologue

Ryan[1] found out just before his sixteenth birthday that he had been selected to serve as one of the Federal Emergency Management Agency (FEMA) Youth Preparedness Council (YPC) representatives for his region of the United States. Although he had always been a high-achieving stu-

The authors would like to thank Stefanie Haeffele and Virgil Henry Storr at the Mercatus Center at George Mason University for their editorial leadership. Nick Horna and Christopher Rini, both undergraduate research assistants at the Natural Hazards Center, assisted with data collection for this chapter. Allison Carlock, National Youth Preparedness Lead at the Federal Emergency Management Agency, reviewed an earlier draft of this chapter, which is gratefully acknowledged. *This material is based upon work supported by the National Science Foundation under grant no. 1635593. Any opinions, findings, and conclusions or recommendations expressed in this material are those of the authors and do not necessarily reflect the views of the National Science Foundation.*

L. Peek (✉) • S. Domingue
Department of Sociology, University of Colorado Boulder, Boulder, CO, USA

Natural Hazards Center, University of Colorado Boulder, Boulder, CO, USA
e-mail: lori.peek@colorado.edu; simone.domingue@colorado.edu

© The Author(s) 2020   **61**
S. Haeffele, V. H. Storr (eds.), *Government Responses to Crisis*, Mercatus Studies
in Political and Social Economy, https://doi.org/10.1007/978-3-030-39309-0_5

dent and involved member of his broader community, Ryan said there was "something really special" about being a member of YPC.

Founded in 2012 to convene youth leaders interested in supporting preparedness efforts and developing a culture of disaster readiness, the YPC typically includes between 10 and 15 youth leaders who are identified through a competitive application process to participate in the program. These YPC members are invited to attend an annual meeting, held in the summer in Washington, DC, where they receive training and mentoring from leading emergency management professionals and child protection experts. During their two-year appointment on the council, all of the YPC members are encouraged to develop and launch their own local- or national-level disaster preparedness project. They are also regularly invited to provide input and a youth perspective on new programs and initiatives.

Ryan—who was raised in a community subject to weather extremes, where it is especially hot and dry in the summer months and extremely cold and snowy in the winter—decided that he wanted to help equip teens with the information, skills, and materials necessary to survive a severe winter storm. His idea for the "Blizzard Bag" was borne out of his belief that teens may be especially vulnerable[2] if they are trapped in their vehicle in freezing weather conditions, and his desire to encourage teens to take action to create their own disaster supply kit so that "new drivers can be ready for about anything."

Ryan made posters, flyers, and a website and participated in a variety of local events where he would encourage awareness of the threat of winter storm conditions and work to influence teens to act to reduce their risk. He gave talks on the Blizzard Bag in his community and even delivered a plenary presentation on his efforts at a national conference. He raised donations so that he could give away some of the necessary but costlier supplies that the kit requires (which includes a gallon of water, warm clothing or a blanket, nonperishable food, a weather radio, flares, a flashlight, a first-aid kit, and an extra cell phone battery or other power source).

As he neared the end of his term of service with the YPC, Ryan estimated that hundreds of teens had created their own Blizzard Bags in response to the program he developed. In reflecting on his service through the YPC, Ryan noted how much it had changed him. He said that for the first time, he "really understood how much of a difference one person can make." He also acknowledged that while it is true that "no one person can do everything, we can all do something together to make the world a safer place." Ryan obviously recognized that his individual actions created positive change. He was quick to point out, however, that he would not have been able to make such a contribution without the guidance and various forms of support provided by FEMA. Although Ryan had thought about disasters previously—some of his extended family members in India were displaced by catastrophic flooding the year before he applied for the YPC program—he did not know what to do to help reduce risk and to get others thinking about simple, concrete steps that they can take to become better prepared. Ryan clearly had the personal motivation and desire to take on a disaster preparedness project, but it was FEMA that provided a formal *structure of opportunity*—here referring to how the chance to gain certain rewards or achieve certain goals is shaped by the ways that society and specific institutions are organized (Cloward and Ohlin 1960)—for him to get involved and make a difference.

5.2   Introduction

Researchers have systematically studied children's reactions to disaster since the 1940s, although interest in both the subfield and practical interventions to reduce children's vulnerability has grown tremendously over the past decade (Pfefferbaum et al. 2012). In fact, a recent meta-review found that nearly half of all studies on children and disaster have been published since 2010, and most of this recent literature has focused on a limited number of large-scale catastrophic events (Peek et al. 2018). The same review also highlighted six major waves of research on children and disaster that have been prevalent over time, including contributions regarding (1) the effects of disaster on children's mental health and behavioral reactions; (2) disaster exposure as it relates to children's physical health and well-being; (3) social vulnerability and sociodemographic characteristics; (4) the role of institutions and socio-ecological context in shaping children's pre- and post-disaster outcomes; (5) resiliency, strengths, and capacities; and (6) children's voices, perspectives, and actions across the disaster lifecycle (Peek et al. 2018, 244).

Just as scholarship has increased and changed in focus over time, so too have the number and range of federal, state, and local programs that concentrate on children and disasters. This institutional trend is, in many ways, aligned with the aforementioned waves (5) and (6) and the associated scholarly emphasis on children's capacities and their actions in disaster risk reduction.

This chapter provides a brief summary of social vulnerability approaches to understanding disaster and then offers an overview and analysis of a number of programs, educational initiatives, and guidance documents created by federal agencies[3] to engage children and child-serving organizations in emergency management. The chapter demonstrates that these "top-down" responses reflect an increasing commitment on the part of the federal government to reduce children's vulnerability in disasters. Additionally, they underscore a rising awareness of children's ability to participate in activities that reduce their own risk. However, as we argue in this chapter, there are many avenues for the federal government to further engage children in long-term recovery, mitigation, and other disaster risk reduction efforts to further bolster their existing capacities and overall community resilience.

5.3   Social Vulnerability, Children, and Disasters

While some initial studies of disasters cast them as equal opportunity events that caused indiscriminate harm, by the mid-1970s, scholars writing from a social vulnerability perspective began to question and challenge the "naturalness" of so-called natural disasters (O'Keefe et al. 1976). These researchers and others who continued to work in the same vein point out that while many disasters are indeed triggered by natural hazards such as tornadoes, earthquakes, or hurricanes, it is actually social, historical, and economic arrangements that determine the scale and scope of disasters and their effects on diverse populations (Tierney 2014; Wisner et al. 2004).

Because disaster risk is distributed in ways that reflect pre-existing inequalities, groups that are marginalized and have less power and fewer resources often have the hardest time preparing for, responding to, and recovering from disaster (Hewitt 1997; Wisner et al. 2004). Entire volumes have been dedicated to exploring the root causes and the consequences of social vulnerability for specific sociodemographic groups, including women, racial and ethnic minorities, low-income persons, persons with disabilities, the elderly, and children (see Phillips et al. 2009; Thomas et al. 2013; Veenema 2018). And while the majority of available social vulnerability scholarship considers how social class, racial and ethnic status, and gender influence pre- and post-disaster outcomes (Cutter et al. 2003; Morrow 1999), recent publications have also focused on how age—especially among the very old and very young—can impair disaster preparedness, response, and recovery (Peek 2013). For example, older adults are at a greater risk of injury or death in disaster (Bourque et al. 2007). Their susceptibility to harm is caused by a number of factors, such as economic and social marginalization that reduces their ability to stockpile food and medicine, receive and interpret warning messages, safely evacuate, find adequate medical care post disaster, and recover financially and emotionally from trauma (Elmore and Brown 2007–2008). Similarly, age also influences the vulnerability of infants and very young children who may be dependent upon others for care in disasters and are more susceptible to deleterious physical health effects following public health emergencies and disasters (Peek et al. 2018).

Federal mission agencies with the responsibility for effectively responding to disasters have clearly been influenced by the social vulnerability scholarship that is now so prevalent in the hazards and disaster field. For instance, the Centers for Disease Control and Prevention (CDC) has a dedicated Vulnerable Populations Officer within the Office of Public Health Preparedness and Response, the Assistant Secretary for Preparedness and Response in the US Department of Health and Human Services (HHS) has a comprehensive collection of resources on access and functional needs, and FEMA developed the Communication, Medical, Independence, Supervision, and Transportation (C-MIST) framework in recognition of potential needs among varying populations in the categories of C-MIST.

Today, it is hard to imagine any emergency planning guidance that does not include recommendations concerning high-risk, high-vulnerability populations (Davis et al. 2018). This is a testament to how far the hazards and disaster field has come since the 1970s, and to how much the science and practice of vulnerability reduction and crisis response has advanced. At the same time, scholars have called for more nuanced and complex disaster management frameworks that recognize interdependencies between broader social and cultural systems and how they intersect with more micro-level behaviors and actions to ultimately influence individual and community capacity (Enarson 2012; Luft 2016; O'Sullivan and Craig 2013). Indeed, this newer wave of social vulnerability scholarship recognizes the utility of naming so-called vulnerable groups to ensure they are not left behind in emergency preparedness planning but also challenges researchers and practitioners to explore how a particular marker of vulnerability intersects with historical and contemporary patterns of inequality (see Table 5.1).

The *recognition* of socially vulnerable groups is a *prerequisite* for the types of more complex and dynamic definitions represented in Table 5.1. This is important to underscore because the marginalization of populations is often what leads to their invisibility in structures of power and opportunity and ultimately drives their vulnerability. It is through the process of naming potentially vulnerable groups that scholars and emergency management professionals can begin to unpack the complex historical and contemporary processes that influence unequal outcomes.

Children, for example, make up nearly 25 percent of the total US population. Yet, before Hurricane Katrina brought their suffering into such sharp relief, they were rarely included or considered in emergency management planning and practice (Peek 2008). Indeed, the presidentially appointed National Commission on Children and Disasters (2010) identified the lack of recognition of children as a distinct population within other "at-risk" populations as a major barrier to prioritizing children's needs in disaster, such as their need for mental health services, pediatric health care, or educational support services. Today, that has changed in many ways, as is evidenced by the rise in scholarship on children's vulnerability and capacities in disaster (Peek et al. 2018) and the ever-growing number of federally focused programs on children, youth, and disasters (FEMA 2016). While these developments are certainly encouraging and indicative of a wider awareness of children's unique needs, as we shall later discuss, there are still many opportunities for top-down disaster responses to better serve children and recognize their capacity to initiate change within their social environments.

Table 5.1 Examples of static versus dynamic and intersectional definitions of social vulnerability

Examples of static indicators of social vulnerability—"The vulnerable populations checklist" model	Examples of dynamic indicators and intersectional lenses for understanding social vulnerability
Children	Age alone does not render a child vulnerable to disaster—except in the case of infants and the youngest children, who may need complete protection and care in the face of disaster. For most children and youth, their vulnerability is influenced by their age as well as by other factors such as family structure; exclusion from the public sphere and from decision-making bodies that influence their lives; a lack of voting rights; cultural systems that devalue the perspectives and ignore the voices of children and youth; stigma or stereotypes against young people; and high rates of child poverty (Marchezini and Trajber 2017; Peek 2008).
Elderly	Age alone does not render a person over the age of 60 or 65—which most societies use to define those who are considered elderly—vulnerable in disaster. Instead, older persons may be more susceptible to harm and suffering in disaster under certain conditions, such as when they: experience physical or medical conditions that limit their mobility; depend on particular devices or medical treatments that require power or access to prescription medications; experience physical disabilities that may limit their ability to receive warnings or to take necessary protective actions; and lack access to the Internet, a computer, or other resources necessary to apply for and receive post-disaster aid (Peek 2013).
Gender	There is nothing inherent about gender that renders women and girls more susceptible to death, injury, or harm in disaster. Instead, patriarchal systems that privilege male perspectives and power generate disparate post-disaster outcomes. In most places around the world, women are less likely to: experience political representation proportionate to their share of the population, sustain financial and social independence, and earn wages and salaries commensurate with their male counterparts. Women and girls are more likely to: experience violence and abuse, be politically and socially marginalized and economically exploited, and live in poverty. It is these factors, and many others, that shape their vulnerability to disaster, not their gender alone (Enarson 2012; Fothergill 2004; Luft 2016).

(continued)

Table 5.1 (continued)

Examples of static indicators of social vulnerability—"The vulnerable populations checklist" model	Examples of dynamic indicators and intersectional lenses for understanding social vulnerability
Racial and ethnic minorities	In the United States, Hispanics/Latinos, Blacks/African Americans, Asians/Asian Americans, and American Indians/Native Americans represent the four largest racial and ethnic minority groups. Taken together, they comprise about one-third of the total US population. Each of these groups has experienced a unique history of overtly racist and discriminatory policies that institutionalized their exclusion and segregation and led to the denial of various resources, rights, and opportunities. Those formal policies and the informal practices associated with them have resulted in centuries of unequal allocation of resources and present-day social, economic, and health disparities. It is these racial fault lines—and nothing inherent about racial and ethnic minority status itself—that actually determine the unequal losses and harm often experienced among racial and ethnic minorities in disasters (Fothergill et al. 1999).
Low-income populations	People living in poverty or near-poverty often have the hardest time mitigating, preparing for, responding to, and recovering from disaster. Low-income populations are more likely to live in the most vulnerable housing and tend to lack the resources necessary to relocate, to elevate, or to retrofit. Where the poor live, and their lack of capacity to mitigate or prepare, can then translate into higher rates of death and injury in disaster, more mental health distress, delayed recovery times, and protracted or permanent displacement (Fothergill and Peek 2004).

Source: Authors' creation

5.4 Top-Down Approaches to Engaging Children and Youth in Disasters: A Summary of Federal Programs

The increased recognition of children's vulnerability has coincided with the development of federal programs, initiatives, and curricular materials aimed at engaging children and youth in understanding and reducing the risks that they may face in their homes, schools, and communities. In this section of the chapter, we describe several illustrative examples of such programs that are explicitly designed for children and youth. We found these materials through conducting internet searches of federal agency websites and using terms such as "children," "youth," and "schools." We also identified programs while reviewing guidance documents from federal entities (FEMA 2016; GAO 2016) and published literature summarizing resilience interventions for children and youth (Abramson et al. 2014; Peek et al. 2018).

Table 5.2 includes a list of current federal-level programs and initiatives focused on children and youth. We reviewed the associated websites, guidance documents, and other materials for these programs and initiatives. We then prepared a brief description of each program, highlighting in bold the phase of the disaster lifecycle (e.g., preparedness, emergency response, recovery, mitigation) that the program is focused on, as well as the target age for the population the program is geared toward.

The resources and educational curriculum described in Table 5.2 cover a range of natural and environmental hazards and focus on different age groups from pre-Kindergarten to beyond high school. Most are designed to actively engage children and youth in understanding the natural hazards and other environmental risks they may face in their community. The programs are often meant to be embedded in existing networks of local organizations such as schools, universities, service clubs, child-serving organizations, and local government.

As emphasized in bold in Table 5.2, almost all of these programs are about educating children and youth and helping them to prepare for and, in some cases, effectively respond during the emergency phase of disaster. For example, FEMA's YPC and Teen CERT program are two initiatives

Table 5.2 Description of federal disaster programs and initiatives focused on engaging children and youth

Program or initiative	Responsible federal agency	Description	Target age
America's PrepareAthon!	Federal Emergency Management Agency (FEMA)	This is a grassroots campaign intended to encourage communities to conduct **preparedness** drills and exercises and have hazards-related discussions. It is sponsored by FEMA, but it is about promoting local action. FEMA provides a number of resources pertaining to how organizations can participate in the event. The campaign is for the whole community, and as such, children and youth are meant to be a part of activities (https://www.fema.gov/media-library/assets/documents/94719).	All ages, families, and schools are encouraged to participate
Ready Kids	FEMA	This is a curriculum for emergency **preparedness** for children and contains additional resources for educators and parents. Interactive games for children and teens focused on building a disaster kit and preparing for various hazards and disasters are included (https://www.ready.gov/kids).	Elementary through high school students
Student Tools for Emergency Planning (STEP)	FEMA	STEP is a classroom-based emergency **preparedness** curriculum where students learn about disasters, emergencies, hazards, and how to create a disaster supply kit and communication plan for their family. Lessons focus on communication plans, building a supply kit, and what to do in fire, severe weather, earthquake, and other hazards (https://www.fema.gov/media-library/assets/documents/110946).	4th- and 5th-grade students
Teen Community Emergency Response Team (Teen CERT)	FEMA	The CERT program trains community members in disaster emergency response skills, such as: fire safety, light search and rescue, team organization, incident command, and disaster medical operations. The purpose of Teen CERT is to train students in emergency preparedness and basic response to ensure that they have the skills needed to protect themselves, and assist others, in the event of emergencies. This program was established to help build **preparedness** and **emergency response** capacities within high schools and among teens (https://www.fema.gov/media-library/resources-documents/collections/481).	High school age students

Youth Preparedness Council	FEMA	This program was created by FEMA to help youth implement disaster preparedness projects. The youth who are selected meet with FEMA staff who provide input on their projects. The members of the council also meet annually for a summit (https://www.ready.gov/youth-preparedness-council).	8th- to 11th-grade students are eligible to apply
Kids Environment: Kids Health	National Institutes of Health (NIH)	This educational, preparedness, and emergency response resource contains links to lessons on over 70 topics related to environmental health, including chemicals, harm prevention, and illness outbreak. The page also has games, activities, and topics that kids and teens can explore (https://kids.niehs.nih.gov/).	Kindergarten to 12th grade and beyond
National Weather Service Education Page	National Weather Service (NWS)	This webpage features links to weather science and weather safety educational materials. Additionally, there are links to interactive games for kids and teens, along with links for parents and educators on preparedness and emergency response for floods, hurricanes, thunderstorms, winter weather, and tornadoes (https://www.weather.gov/owlie/).	All ages
StormReady	NWS	This is a certification preparedness program that requires that to be "officially StormReady," a community must: establish a 24-hour warning point and emergency operations center, have more than one way to receive severe weather warnings and forecasts and to alert the public, create a system that monitors weather conditions locally, promote the importance of public readiness through community seminars, and develop a formal hazardous weather plan that includes training severe weather spotters and holding emergency exercises (https://www.weather.gov/stormready/).	Encourages participation of the whole community, with an emphasis on participation from schools ranging from pre-school to high school

(continued)

Table 5.2 (continued)

Program or initiative	Responsible federal agency	Description	Target age
Ready Wrigley	Centers for Disease Control and Protection (CDC)	Ready Wrigley is a dog that also serves as a public health **preparedness** mascot. Ready Wrigley educational resources include books in English and Spanish on preparedness for extreme weather, flu, earthquakes, tornados, and floods, and an app that teaches children about preparedness and response (https://www.cdc.gov/phpr/readywrigley/index.htm).	Ages 2–8 years
Medical Reserve Corps (MRC)	US Department of Health and Human Services (HHS)	This is a program for volunteers who want to get engaged with **preparedness** and **emergency response**. Approximately 22 percent of MRC units across the county let youth join or have Junior MRC units. MRC units often support and supplement youth health education programs like CPR and first aid training (https://mrc.hhs.gov/HomePage).	Ages 5 years to adult
Recipes for Healthy Kids and a Healthy Environment	US Environmental Protection Agency (EPA)	This educational and **preparedness** curriculum includes lessons on environmental health, pests and household hazards, air quality, sun protection, and climate change (https://www.epa.gov/children/student-curriculum).	Ages 9–13 years
Earthquakes for Kids	US Geological Survey (USGS)	This page contains links for earthquake educational materials that are designed for children, including science fair projects and earthquake facts. This page also contains links to **preparedness** documents and resources, like the "Great ShakeOut Earthquake Drills" webpage (https://earthquake.usgs.gov/learn/kids/).	All ages

Source: Authors' creation

that involve teens in keeping their schools and families safe by encouraging them to disseminate their knowledge of disaster preparedness and response to their families and social networks and by encouraging them to take action in disaster situations (FEMA 2012). These programs are based on the principle that active participation from youth is critical to cultivating their ability to effectively respond to emergencies and leads to better post-disaster outcomes (Flint and Stevenson 2010).

5.5 Top-Down Approaches to Engaging Adults and Organizations in Child-Focused Risk Reduction: A Summary of Federal Guidance

While the resources described in Table 5.2 are designed to engage children and youth in emergency management, our search also yielded several additional published reports, framework documents, training modules, factsheets, and other materials prepared by federal mission agencies for adult leaders and professionals. Specifically, we found a number of federal guidance documents geared toward emergency managers, school administrators, childcare providers, and other persons and groups responsible for preparing children, families, and child-serving institutions for disaster.

Table 5.3 lists and briefly describes federal resources and guidance documents aimed toward adults and organizational leaders regarding children and disasters. In each program description, we highlight in bold the phase of the disaster lifecycle (e.g., preparedness, emergency response, recovery, mitigation) that the information is focused on, and we also include a brief statement on the target audience. Taken together, these documents (1) describe the range of vulnerabilities that may be experienced by children and youth, (2) provide guidance for incorporating children and youth into disaster planning, (3) promote cross-sector collaboration and partnership building to address children's needs in disasters, and (4) offer strategies for mitigating hazards risk, implementing educational programs, and promoting preparedness and recovery among children.

Table 5.3 Summary of available federal guidance documents for adults and focused on children, youth, and disasters

Name of document	Responsible federal agency or agencies	Description	Audience
Multihazard Planning for Childcare	Federal Emergency Management Agency (FEMA)	This course material is for childcare providers developing multi-hazards **preparedness** plans (https://training.fema.gov/emiweb/is36/student%20manual/is-36_complete_sm_feb2012.pdf).	Childcare providers
Preparedness Tips for School Administrators	FEMA	This factsheet includes disaster **preparedness** resources for school administrators, emphasizing keeping children and teens safe in schools during disaster (https://www.fema.gov/media-library/assets/documents/30509).	School administrators
Safer, Stronger, Smarter: A Guide to Improving School Natural Hazard Safety	FEMA	This guidebook focuses on safe building standards, structural **mitigation**, emergency **preparedness**, and long-term **recovery** planning for schools (https://www.fema.gov/media-library/assets/documents/132592).	Primary: school administrators, teachers, school safety advocates, and emergency managers Secondary: parents and school children
Youth Preparedness Catalog: Disaster Preparedness Programs and Resources	FEMA	This catalog provides a comprehensive and regularly updated summary of national, state, and local programs on youth **preparedness** education (https://www.fema.gov/media-library/assets/documents/94775).	Persons or organizations involved in youth preparedness programs
Youth Preparedness: Implementing a Community Based Program	FEMA	This document helps guide communities and community-based organizations in developing and implementing youth **preparedness** programs (https://www.ready.gov/youth-preparedness).	Community-based organizations

Helping Children and Adolescents Cope with Violence and Disaster: What Parents Can Do?	National Institutes of Health (NIH)	This document provides an overview of children's vulnerability to trauma and describes the potential short- and longer-term impacts of trauma on mental health. It also outlines steps to help children cope during the **emergency response** and **recovery** phase (https://www.nimh.nih.gov/health/publications/helping-children-and-adolescents-cope-with-violence-and-disasters-parents/index.shtml).	Parents with children exposed to violence or disaster
Caring for Children in Disaster	Centers for Disease Control and Prevention (CDC)	Webpage content discusses why children are vulnerable in disasters, how to help children cope in emergencies, and how to plan for **all stages** of emergency, and describes specific threats to children (https://www.cdc.gov/childrenindisasters/index.html).	General public, teachers, childcare professionals, families, health professionals, and emergency planners
Emergency Preparedness and Children: Protecting our Future	CDC	This issue brief contains a short summary of children's vulnerability in emergencies and offers advice for emergency **preparedness** actions (https://www.cdc.gov/phpr/whatwedo/children.htm).	General public
Planning for an Emergency: Strategies for Identifying and Engaging At-Risk Groups: A Guidance Document for Emergency Managers	CDC	This document outlines steps for defining at-risk groups, locating at-risk groups before disaster strikes, and reaching at-risk groups, including children, during the emergency **preparedness** phase (https://rems.ed.gov/docs/REMS_K-12_Guide_508.pdf).	Emergency managers and planners

(continued)

Table 5.3 (continued)

Name of document	Responsible federal agency or agencies	Description	Audience
Identification and Engagement of Socially Vulnerable Populations in the USACE Decision Making Process	US Army Corps of Engineers (USACE)	This document outlines strategies for identifying and engaging populations that are vulnerable to environmental hazards, including children and youth, during the emergency **preparedness and planning** phase of the emergency management lifecycle (https://www.iwr.usace.army.mil/Portals/70/docs/iwrreports/Identifying_and_Engaging_Socially_Vulnerable_Populations_%20IWRv2_08_01_2016.pdf?ver=2016-08-11-125141-427).	USACE personnel and other government agencies
Practical Information on Crisis Planning: A Guide for Schools and Communities	US Department of Education (ED)	This guidance document lists action items across **all stages** of the disaster lifecycle for stakeholders to consider when developing crisis plans (https://rems.ed.gov/docs/PracticalInformationonCrisisPlanning.pdf).	Schools, school districts, local communities
Children and Youth Task Force in Disasters: Guidelines for Development	US Department of Health and Human Services (HHS)	This document introduces community partners to the Children and Youth Task Force Model. The document includes case studies and explains the role of HHS departments in providing support during **emergency response** and in public health emergencies (https://www.acf.hhs.gov/ohsepr/resource/children-and-youth-task-force-in-disasters).	States, tribes, territories, local communities
Protecting Children's Health During and After Disaster	US Environmental Protection Agency (EPA)	This page lists information on children's health in the **emergency response** and **recovery** period after floods, extreme heat, and wildfires/volcanic ash events (https://www.epa.gov/children/protecting-childrens-health-during-and-after-natural-disasters).	General public, local, state, and federal agencies, and healthcare providers

National Strategy for Youth Preparedness Education: Empowering, Educating, and Building Resilience	FEMA, the American Red Cross, and ED	This document outlines a strategy for catalyzing youth **preparedness** programs and building partnerships among stakeholders involved in disaster planning (https://www.fema.gov/media-library/assets/documents/96107).	Child-serving organizations, local government, federal agencies, non-profit organizations
Guide for Developing High-Quality School Emergency Operations Plans	ED, HHS, Department of Homeland Security (DHS), Department of Justice (DOJ), Federal Bureau of Investigation (FBI), FEMA	This document offers comprehensive guidance for creating and implementing school emergency operations plans. The document focuses primarily on **emergency preparedness** and **emergency response** (https://rems.ed.gov/docs/REMS_K-12_Guide_508.pdf).	School leaders, emergency managers, other partners involved in school emergency response planning
The Impacts of Climate Change on Human Health in the United States: Populations of Concern	EPA, HHS, National Oceanic and Atmospheric Administration (NOAA)	This scientific assessment discusses the vulnerability of different populations, including children, to climate-related hazards and the potential impacts of a range of climate stressors on human health and well-being. The document offers recommendations for identifying vulnerable populations during the emergency preparedness phase and effectively mobilizing in **emergency response** (https://health2016.globalchange.gov/).	Policy makers, public, government agencies

(continued)

Table 5.3 (continued)

Name of document	Responsible federal agency or agencies	Description	Audience
Post-Disaster Childcare Needs and Resources	Interagency Working Group	This document catalogs resources available to communities, states, and childcare providers for **preparedness** and **planning**, **emergency response**, and **recovery**, highlighting potential gaps for in care for families and childcare providers (https://www.acf.hhs. gov/sites/default/files/ohsepr/post_disaster_child_care_ planning_matrix_11mar2016_final.pdf).	States, childcare providers, community members
Post-Disaster Reunification of Children: A Nationwide Approach	FEMA, HHS	This document describes the coordination processes associated with reunifying unaccompanied minors with their parents or legal guardians during the **emergency response** phase and following a large-scale disaster (https://www.fema.gov/media-library/assets/ documents/85559).	State and local governments, community stakeholders and leaders

Source: Authors' creation

The resources and guidance documents described in Table 5.3 address various human-caused threats and natural and environmental hazards. They also cover a range of potential impacts to children, families, childcare providers, schools, and communities. Because these documents are geared toward adults who are parents, childcare providers, school administrators, emergency managers, or community leaders, they aim to increase understanding of children's vulnerability while also promoting action to reduce that vulnerability.

As emphasized in bold in Table 5.3, these websites, reports, and guidance documents span the disaster lifecycle, focusing on emergency preparedness, response, recovery, and mitigation. As with the child-centered emergency management curriculum summarized in Table 5.2, most of the documents included in Table 5.3 also focus on the emergency preparedness and planning phase of the disaster lifecycle. In addition, a few of the documents also consider the early- and longer-term stages of recovery, and what actions adults might take to help children to cope and adjust after a potentially traumatic event. Notably, the FEMA (2017) *Safer, Stronger, Smarter* guidebook is the only document represented in Table 5.3 that is explicitly concerned with mitigation actions intended to ensure the structural integrity of schools and other buildings that children might occupy during the school day.

5.6 Analysis of Gaps and Opportunities for Federal Guidance on Children and Disasters

With the rise of social vulnerability research, federal agencies have clearly recognized children as a potentially vulnerable group in disaster. Furthermore, these agencies have made tremendous strides in offering educational curriculum and other materials for involving children in disaster preparedness and emergency response efforts through interactive educational opportunities that build skills and seek to reduce harms caused by disaster. In addition, the federal government now offers a wide variety of guidance documents to adult leaders and formal organizations regarding child-centered needs in disaster preparedness, response, and recovery.

Although much progress has been made, especially since Hurricane Katrina devastated the US Gulf Coast in 2005, some important gaps remain regarding both the *participatory nature* and the *content* of these initiatives. We believe, however, that these gaps present opportunities for strengthening the federal government's commitment to risk reduction, child and youth empowerment, and community resilience.

The educational programs in Table 5.2 differed in the degree to which they provide *formal structures of opportunities* (Cloward and Ohlin 1960), as described in the opening vignette to this chapter. The YPC represents a high standard in this regard, in that it allows teens like Ryan to actively engage in risk reduction by giving them the opportunity to design their own projects. Furthermore, this program also provides the tools and material resources to act on their ideas for risk reduction. This allows for the "co-production" of public services (Parks et al. 1981) by fostering buy-in and utilizing local knowledge that can be applied to ensure risk reduction is effective. For instance, Ryan's Blizzard Bag project was designed around his insight that first-time drivers who are teenagers are especially vulnerable to severe winter weather. FEMA then provided him the requisite mentorship and support to implement a program based on his passion and commitment to emergency planning.

A growing body of research has shown that children are especially adept at recognizing key drivers of disaster vulnerability and of identifying innovative approaches to building community resilience (Ronan and Johnston 2005). Far from being scared or intimidated by hazards-related information, children and youth repeatedly express a strong desire to know more about the risks in their environment and to actively engage to reduce those threats (Towers et al. 2014). Thus, we see an opportunity for the federal government to continue to provide resources and leadership regarding the active engagement of children and youth across the disaster lifecycle.

However, to date, most of the programs for children and youth draw upon a model of personal preparedness (as opposed to collective empowerment) and focus on emergency planning and response (as opposed to the entire emergency management lifecycle). Indeed, the programs represented in Table 5.2 for children and youth emphasized understanding and reducing their individual risk and aiding in the immediate aftermath of disaster. Federal guidance documents that targeted adults, as shown in Table 5.3, as the primary stakeholders in disaster risk reduction addressed organizational and institutional dynamics that are critical to reducing vulnerability. For example, the FEMA (2017) guidebook *Safer, Stronger, Smarter* explicitly addressed hazards mitigation—or activities meant to reduce the long-term risk to people or properties in disaster (Mileti 1999). Children and youth were not the primary audience for this extensive guidebook, although as the authors note, "parents, caregivers, and students" can use the guide to "advocate for safe schools in their communities" (FEMA 2017, 1–6). We argue that the lack of engaging, interactive, child- and youth-friendly mitigation programs represents a serious oversight in terms of top-down interventions for young people. Examples of structural hazards mitigation activities include retrofitting unreinforced masonry schools located in earthquake country, elevating homes located in floodplains, installing tsunami evacuation structures, and building storm shelters or safe rooms in tornado-prone regions. Mitigation actions, especially those that require new legislation or policies, or that require changes in engineering or urban planning practice, can be costly, time-consuming, and politically challenging to implement. But mitigation is also perhaps the single most important activity that individuals and communities can take to reduce economic losses and other consequences from disasters (Multihazard Mitigation Council 2017). As such, it is crucial that children and youth be educated about the importance of mitigation and collectively empowered to engage in activities that can help make their homes, schools, and communities safe from hazards.

Recovery, here defined as children regaining or attaining stability in all the spheres of their lives (family, housing, education, extracurricular activities, peer groups, and health care) after a disaster (Fothergill and Peek 2015), was also significantly underrepresented in the child- and adult-specific programs and initiatives that we reviewed. Recovery was nevertheless recognized as a key concern for children and youth (for example, see NIH 2015). In 2017, the costliest disaster loss year in US history, millions of Americans were directly affected in disasters. In the case of the most catastrophic events, recovery may take years, if not decades. With the increased frequency and magnitude of US disasters, the lack of focus on long-term recovery also represents an opportunity for engaging children and youth in helping to foster their own and others recovery through interactive peer listening programs, problem-based learning curricular activities, and other initiatives that engage cycles of disaster impact, recovery, and rebuilding. Similarly, it is important to recognize that child-serving institutions such as childcare centers, schools, and child-friendly spaces such as parks and playgrounds may be slow to recover after disaster and may require additional resources. This is worthy of further top-down focus and guidance from the federal level.

An additional gap that we recognized in our review was regarding acknowledgment of the diversity of children and youth. Now that this group is on the radar as a potentially vulnerable population, it is crucial that top-down guidance adopt an intersectional lens that is attentive to age-based differences in vulnerabilities and capacities, as well as other forms of diversity that children experience. Most of the guidance documents treated children as a monolithic group, as opposed to a dynamic category of people marked by difference in terms of racial and ethnic status, gender identity, sexual orientation, immigration status, family income, and family structure.

5.7   Conclusion

This chapter offered a summary of federal initiatives and programs that recognize children's vulnerability to negative physical, psychological, and educational impacts of disaster (Peek 2008), while also acknowledging their capacity to meaningfully contribute to disaster readiness and response. Additionally, this chapter has identified key gaps and opportunities for federal leadership in the children and disasters space.

We see the implications of this chapter as twofold. First, we argue that the federal-level recognition and acknowledgment of children and youth as a vulnerable population in disasters is exceptionally important, in that it renders this group *visible* in disaster planning and response. The visibility of this group is crucial not only because they make up nearly one-quarter of the total population of the United States, but also because they have unique needs that will only be met once they are identified and resources are allocated to react accordingly.

Second, the education and empowerment of children and youth as well as of adults who care for and educate young people is a first step toward vulnerability reduction. The programs and initiatives represented in Table 5.2 and the guidance documents described in Table 5.3 are all about recognizing children's vulnerability and then acting to reduce that vulnerability.

Even with the progress that has been made in this space, we take the stance that there are opportunities for further improvement and leadership from the federal government. Specifically, we see a need for more formal structures of opportunity that engage children and youth in designing their own paths to risk reduction. We also call for more programs and initiatives that move beyond emergency preparedness and response to more meaningfully encompass hazards mitigation and long-term recovery. Finally, as federal agencies continue to invest in the development of programs for children and youth and of documents for adults who care for these populations, it is crucial that this guidance recognize the diversity of this population.

Ensuring that educational curriculum, child-centered programs, and vulnerability reduction initiatives generated by the federal government focus on the entire disaster lifecycle—from preparedness, to emergency response, to recovery, to mitigation—and on empowering the diverse generation of children and youth who are coming of age in an ever more turbulent world will serve everyone for the better. Moreover, widening the opportunities for children to take part in activities across the disaster lifecycle represents one powerful means of addressing the dynamic nature of their vulnerability.

Notes

1. Ryan is a pseudonym. The lead author for this chapter served as one of his mentors and that is how we learned of his journey and engagement with the Youth Preparedness Council.
2. Ryan's assumption regarding the lethality of winter storms among those in his age group was correct. Excessive cold associated with severe winter

weather kills more 15- to 24-year-old people in the United States than any other natural hazard (see Zahran et al. 2008).

3. Although there are local and state government initiatives on children and disasters, as well as many programs available through private, non-profit, and academic sectors, this chapter analyzes federal initiatives. Our rationale for this focus is twofold. First, this edited volume is organized around top-down initiatives in crisis management, and therefore, we sought to review children and disaster programs released from the highest level of government. Second, given time and space constraints, we were not able to complete a comprehensive review for all states and localities across the United States or for all sectors. Various federal agencies do, however, offer comprehensive lists of resources on children, youth, and disasters such as those available from the US Department of Health and Human Services (https://www.acf.hhs.gov/ohsepr/children-and-families), the Centers for Disease Control and Prevention (https://www.cdc.gov/childrenindisasters/index.html), and the Federal Emergency Management Agency (https://www.fema.gov/children-and-disasters).

References

Abramson, D., K. Brooks, and L. Peek. 2014. The Science and Practice of Resilience Interventions for Children Exposed to Disasters. In *Preparedness, Response, and Recovery Considerations for Children and Families: Workshop Summary*, ed. T. Wizemann, M. Reeve, and B.M. Altevogt, 177–202. Washington, DC: The National Academies Press.

Bourque, L.B., J.M. Siegel, M. Kano, and M.M. Wood. 2007. Morbidity and Mortality Associated with Disasters. In *Handbook of Disaster Research*, ed. H. Rodríguez, E.L. Quarantelli, and R.R. Dynes, 97–112. New York: Springer.

Cloward, R.A., and L.E. Ohlin. 1960. *Delinquency and Opportunity: A Theory of Delinquent Gangs*. Glencoe: The Free Press.

Cutter, S.L., B.J. Boruff, and W.L. Shirley. 2003. Social Vulnerability to Environmental Hazards. *Social Science Quarterly* 84 (2): 242–261.

Davis, E.A., R. Hansen, L. Peek, B. Phillips, and S. Tuneberg. 2018. Identifying and Accommodating High-Risk, High-Vulnerability Populations in Disasters. In *Disaster Nursing and Emergency Preparedness for Chemical, Biological, and Radiological Terrorism and Other Hazards*, ed. T.G. Veenema, 4th ed., 115–138. New York: Springer.

Elmore, D., and L. Brown. 2007–2008. Emergency Preparedness and Response: Health and Social Policy Implications for Older Adults. *Generations* 4 (Winter): 66–74.

Enarson, E. 2012. *Women Confronting Natural Disaster: From Vulnerability to Resilience.* Boulder, CO: Lynne Rienner Publishers.

FEMA. 2012. *Teen CERT Guide: Launching and Maintaining the Training.* Washington, DC: Federal Emergency Management Agency.

———. 2016. *Youth Preparedness Catalog: Disaster Preparedness Programs and Resources.* Washington, DC: Federal Emergency Management Agency.

———. 2017. *Safer, Stronger, Smarter: A Guide to Improving School Natural Hazard Safety.* FEMA P-1000. Washington, DC: Federal Emergency Management Agency.

Flint, C.G., and J. Stevenson. 2010. Building Community Disaster Preparedness with Volunteers: Community Emergency Response Teams in Illinois. *Natural Hazards Review* 11 (3): 118–124.

Fothergill, A. 2004. *Heads Above Water: Gender, Class, and Family in the Grand Forks Flood.* Albany, NY: SUNY Press.

Fothergill, A., and L. Peek. 2004. Poverty and Disasters in the United States: A Review of Recent Sociological Findings. *Natural Hazards* 32 (1): 89–110.

———. 2015. *Children of Katrina.* Austin: University of Texas Press.

Fothergill, A., E.G.M. Maestas, and J.D. Darlington. 1999. Race, Ethnicity and Disasters in the United States: A Review of the Literature. *Disasters* 23 (2): 156–173.

GAO. 2016. *Emergency Management: Improved Federal Coordination Could Better Assist K-12 Schools Prepare for Emergencies, Report to Congressional Requesters.* GAO-16-144. Washington, DC: Government Accountability Office.

Hewitt, K. 1997. *Regions of Risk: A Geographical Introduction to Disasters.* Boston: Addison Wesley Longman.

Luft, R.E. 2016. Disaster Patriarchy: An Intersectional Model for Understanding Disaster at the Ten-Year Anniversary of Hurricane Katrina. *Feminist Formations* 28 (2): 1–26.

Marchezini, V., and R. Trajber. 2017. Youth-Based Learning in Disaster Risk Reduction Education. In *Responses to Disasters and Climate Change: Understanding Vulnerability and Fostering Resilience*, ed. M. Companion and M.S. Chaiken. Boca Raton, FL: CRC Press.

Mileti, D.S. 1999. *Disasters by Design: A Reassessment of Natural Hazards in the United States.* Washington, DC: Joseph Henry Press.

Morrow, B.H. 1999. Identifying and Mapping Community Vulnerability. *Disasters* 23 (1): 1–18.

Multihazard Mitigation Council. 2017. *Natural Hazard Mitigation Saves 2017 Interim Report: An Independent Study*. Principal Investigator: Keith Porter; Co-Principal Investigators: Scawthorn, C., Dash, N., Santos, J.; Investigators: Eguchi, M., Ghosh, M.S., Huyck, C., Isteita, M., Mickey, K., Rashed, T., Schneider, P. Director, MMC. Washington, DC: National Institute of Building Sciences, Multihazard Mitigation Council.

National Commission on Children and Disasters. 2010. *Report to the President and Congress*. AHRQ Publication No. 10-M037. Rockville: Agency for Healthcare Research and Quality.

NIH. 2015. *Helping Children and Adolescents Cope with Violence and Disasters: What Parents Can Do*. NIH Publication No. 15-3518. Washington, DC: National Institutes of Health.

O'Keefe, P., K. Westgate, and B. Wisner. 1976. Taking the Naturalness Out of Natural Disasters. *Nature* 260: 566–567.

O'Sullivan, T.L., and E. Craig. 2013. Unraveling the Complexities of Disaster Management: A Framework for Critical Social Infrastructure to Promote Population Health and Resilience. *Social Science and Medicine* 93: 238–246.

Parks, R., P. Baker, L. Kiser, R. Oakerson, E. Ostrom, S. Percy, M. Vandivort, G. Whitaker, and R. Wilson. 1981. Consumers as Producers of Public Services: Some Economic and Institutional Considerations. In *Polycentricity and Local Public Economies: Readings from the Workshop in Political Theory and Policy Analysis*, ed. M. McGinnis, 381–391. Ann Arbor: The University of Michigan Press.

Peek, L. 2008. Children and Disasters: Understanding Vulnerability, Developing Capacities, and Promoting Resilience. *Children, Youth, and Environments* 18: 1–29.

———. 2013. Age. In *Social Vulnerability to Disasters*, ed. D.S.K. Thomas, B.D. Phillips, W.E. Lovekamp, and A. Fothergill, 2nd ed., 167–198. Boca Raton: CRC Press.

Peek, L., D. Abramson, R. Cox, A. Fothergill, and J. Tobin. 2018. Children and Disasters. In *Handbook of Disaster Research*, ed. H. Rodriguez, W. Donner, and J.E. Trainor, 2nd ed., 243–262. New York: Springer.

Pfefferbaum, R.L., A.K. Jacobs, B.J. Pfefferbaum, M.A. Noffsinger, K. Sherrieb, and F.H. Norris. 2012. The Burden of Disaster: Part II, Applying Interventions Across the Child's Social Ecology. *International Journal of Emergency Mental Health* 14 (3): 175–187.

Phillips, B.D., D.S.K. Thomas, A. Fothergill, and L. Blinn-Pike, eds. 2009. *Social Vulnerability to Disasters*. Boca Raton: CRC Press.

Ronan, K., and D. Johnston. 2005. *Promoting Community Resilience in Disasters: The Role for Schools, Youth, and Families*. New York: Springer Science and Business Media.

Thomas, D.S.K., B.D. Phillips, W.E. Lovekamp, and A. Fothergill, eds. 2013. *Social Vulnerability to Disasters*. 2nd ed. Boca Raton: CRC Press.

Tierney, K. 2014. *The Social Roots of Risk: Producing Disasters, Promoting Resilience*. Stanford: Stanford Business Books.

Towers, B., K. Haynes, F. Sewell, H. Bailie, and D. Cross. 2014. Child-Centered Disaster Risk Reduction in Australia: Progress, Gaps and Opportunities. *Australian Journal of Emergency Management* 29 (1): 31–38.

Veenema, T.G., ed. 2018. *Disaster Nursing and Emergency Preparedness for Chemical, Biological, and Radiological Terrorism and Other Hazards*. 4th ed. New York: Springer.

Wisner, B., P. Blaikie, T. Cannon, and I. Davis. 2004. *At Risk: Natural Hazards, People's Vulnerability, and Disasters*. 2nd ed. New York: Routledge.

Zahran, S., L. Peek, and S.D. Brody. 2008. Youth Mortality by Forces of Nature. *Children, Youth, and Environments* 18 (1): 371–388.

6

The Political Economy of Foreign Intervention

Christopher J. Coyne and Garrett Wood

6.1 Introduction

Foreign interventions occur when the government in one society attempts to fix perceived problems in another society, substituting the interveners' preferred state of affairs for the existing state of affairs. As the world's dominant economic and political force, the decision makers in the US government have historically employed foreign interventions to address a range of crises in a top-down manner. These include addressing humanitarian crises through aid (both short- and long-term aid) and military

C. J. Coyne (✉)
Department of Economics, George Mason University, Fairfax, VA, USA

F. A. Hayek Program for Advanced Study in Philosophy, Politics, and Economics, Mercatus Center at George Mason University, Fairfax, VA, USA
e-mail: ccoyne3@gmu.edu

G. Wood
Department of Economics, Virginia Wesleyan University, Virginia Beach, VA, USA
e-mail: gwood@vwu.edu

© The Author(s) 2020
S. Haeffele, V. H. Storr (eds.), *Government Responses to Crisis*, Mercatus Studies in Political and Social Economy, https://doi.org/10.1007/978-3-030-39309-0_6

89

force, engaging in post-conflict reconstruction, engaging in state-building, and addressing a wide range of security issues such as terrorism.

US-led foreign interventions are nuanced and often involve multiple, overlapping activities. For example, foreign intervention in response to humanitarian crises often involves the provision of short-term aid to address immediate concerns, the provision of long-term aid to foster development, state-building to resolve political differences and develop quality political institutions, and the use of military to provide security and combat threats. As this example illustrates, foreign interventions often involve some mix of the military, aid and assistance, and diplomacy.

The complexities of US-led foreign interventions are captured by the rise of the "3D" approach which involves a mix of defense (military), diplomacy, and development. This approach is intended to combine the capabilities and strengths of all forms of US influence in order to quell violence, establish representative governments, protect property rights, and spur economic growth (see Coyne 2011). The US government's integrated approach to foreign intervention was captured by former secretary of defense Robert Gates (2009, 31) who argued that the United States needs a "military whose ability to kick down the door is matched by its ability to clean up the mess and even rebuild the house afterward." In this context, rebuilding the house involves more than just physically reconstructing infrastructure and instead entails the rebuilding all aspects of societies—economic, legal, social, political—by employing an array of tools—humanitarian and development aid, force, training—that integrate the various functions of the US government.

The purpose of this chapter is to highlight some of the key constraints facing foreign interventions as a top-down method of addressing crises. Specific focus is placed on the epistemic and political economy issues relevant to foreign intervention. These constraints must be critically considered in order to determine if foreign intervention is a viable solution to crises. The specific manifestation of these constraints will vary depending on the context in which foreign interventions take place. For example, the constraints facing those involved in the delivery of short-term humanitarian aid in one society will differ greatly from those facing efforts to engage in widespread nation-building in a different society.

Nonetheless, the general categories discussed here are useful in identifying the types of constraints that interveners face.

We proceed as follows. Section 6.2 discusses four manifestations of the knowledge problem in foreign interventions. Section 6.3 considers the incentives created by political institutions and how they constrain foreign intervention. Section 6.4 concludes.

6.2 Knowledge Problems

Interveners may know what outcomes they want to bring about, but that does not mean that they know how to create those outcomes. Knowledge of key variables or ideal institutions is distinct from the dispersed and local knowledge that those variables and structures require to operate and persist. Hayek (1945, 521) described this local knowledge as "the knowledge of the particular circumstances of time and place" which is, by its tacit nature, difficult to centralize and comprehend in any kind of meaningful manner. Foreign interventions will encounter several types of knowledge problems (Coyne 2008a, 2013; Coyne and Pellillo 2011; Duncan and Coyne 2015).

6.2.1 The Knowledge Problem over Institutions

Many foreign interventions purport to create, or contribute to creating, liberal democratic institutions. A central issue facing policymakers and occupiers is the fundamental knowledge problem of how to establish the institutional foundations of a liberal society (Coyne 2008a; Coyne and Pellillo 2011). Many agree on the general characteristics of a free society—protection of individual and property rights, freedom of speech, rule of law, and so on—but the knowledge of how to effectively design and implement these general institutions in specific settings is lacking.

The lack of general knowledge is captured in the following list of propositions regarding what scholars know regarding the emergence of democratic institutions:

1. there are few preconditions for the emergence of democracy,
2. no single factor is sufficient or necessary to the emergence of democracy,
3. the emergence of democracy in a country is the result of a combination of causes,
4. the causes responsible for the emergence of democracy are not the same as those promoting its consolidation,
5. the combination of causes promoting democratic transition and consolidation varies from country to country, and
6. the combination of causes generally responsible for one wave of democratization differs from those responsible for other waves. (Shin 1994, 151)

This lack of general knowledge, about democracy in general, is compounded by the lack of context-specific knowledge regarding traditions, historical experiences, and cultural nuances.

Success in foreign intervention is not simply a matter of taking the rules that work in one society and imposing them on another society (see Boettke 2001, 248–265; Boettke et al. 2008; Coyne 2008a). The ability to transport rules between societies is constrained by the fact that underlying belief systems, values, and ideals often differ across societies. What works in the United States will not work in the Middle East, just like what worked in Japan and West Germany following World War II is a very poor guide for current and future foreign interventions (see Coyne 2008a).

Treatments of foreign intervention often focus on the amount of "effort" in the form of time spent planning, monetary and physical aid, troop levels, the timing of elections, and exit strategy. Unfortunately, this overlooks the deeper issue—whether interveners have the relevant knowledge to achieve their desired ends. To the extent the knowledge over institutions is lacking, it places hard constraints on what foreign intervention can accomplish.

6.2.2 The Knowledge Problem Within Institutions

In addition to attempting to reform or create institutions, foreign interventions often seek to achieve a variety of goals within institutions. Even in seemingly simple situations, however, such as in the delivery of pre-existing humanitarian goods, an intervener's efforts can be frustrated by a lack of local knowledge.

For example, in areas that lack lifesaving medical devices the solution to the problem would seem to be to transfer medical devices from wealthy countries to those in need. Such a solution was attempted at Uganda's Mulago National Referral Hospital and Bwindi Community Hospital (Miesen 2013), with foreigners donating incubators and anesthesia machines that both hospitals were lacking. However, some shipped with instructions in a language that the recipients did not speak and a majority of the incubators broke in a short timeframe. The donor's plans did not anticipate the need for spare parts, repair services, or support staff for these machines. Absent these necessary, complementary goods and services, the donated machines were worthless.

Further compounding the problem is the dynamic nature of local knowledge and expectations. Knowledge and expectations are not static, but instead, are constantly changing and evolving. This has important implications. Outsiders often lack local knowledge because of their epistemic distance from those they are intervening upon. But locals may also lack accurate knowledge and expectations either because of the fluidity of the situation in which they are embedded, or because they lack access to the appropriate information gatekeepers who do understand the "on-the-ground" nuances.

As interventions become more complex, so too do the knowledge problems. Increasing pre-determined outputs, such as medical devices, is one challenge, but creating genuine, widespread development is a much larger challenge. Pritchett and Woolcock (2004, 197), for instance, note that "valuable local 'practices'—idiosyncratic knowledge of variables crucial to the welfare of the poor (e.g. soil conditions, weather patterns, water flows)—get squeezed out, even lost completely, in large centralized development programs."

Beyond the loss of knowledge regarding local practices, there is an even more fundamental issue which is that interveners lack the knowledge necessary to create genuine development. Economic development requires the allocation, and reallocation, of scarce resources to their highest-valued uses (Coyne 2013, 71–79). The information necessary to resolve the economics problem, such that scarce resources are allocated to their highest-valued uses, does not exist outside of markets owing to the absence of economic calculation (Mises [1920] 1935, [1949] 1996; Hayek 1945; Lavoie 1985a, 1985b, 1986). This implies that outside of markets there exists a significant knowledge problem whereby decision makers must allocate scarce resources without the advantage of market prices and profit-and-loss accounting to compare the expected value-added of alternative uses.

This problem plagues central economic planning efforts, of which foreign intervention is one manifestation. Since the allocation of resources in foreign interventions takes place outside of competitive private markets, this necessarily implies that interveners face this knowledge problem and therefore they cannot hope to solve the economic problem of allocating scarce resources in a welfare-maximizing manner.

Appreciating this manifestation of the knowledge problem has important implications for understanding the limits of foreign interventions. Because planning outside of markets cannot solve the economic problem, it cannot replicate the ability of markets to foster societal economic progress. Interveners can potentially increase the amount of certain predetermined outputs, but they cannot solve the economic problem required to achieve economic progress. This places hard constraints on what foreign interventions can hope to achieve (Coyne 2013, 61–89).

6.2.3 The Knowledge Problem and Unintended Consequences

One of the prerequisites for successful intervention is the ability of planners to anticipate potential responses to their actions. This poses a challenge, however, because interveners have limited knowledge about the world which is characterized by an array of overlapping complex systems (Coyne 2013, 147–151). The result is the emergence of negative unintended consequences which fall into four categories.

The first deals with the perverse impact of foreign assistance on the recipient government. Numerous studies indicate that external assistance increases corruption and decreases the quality of political institutions in the recipient countries through distortions to the public sector, delayed reforms, and more rent-seeking for the windfall profits created by the foreign assistance (see Svensson 2000; Knack 2001; Djankov et al. 2006; Hodler 2007).

The second category relates to how foreign interventions affect citizen-recipients by changing the payoffs they face. For example, assistance can have a "dependency effect" whereby recipients become reliant on continued assistance in future periods. This paradox, which has been termed the "Samaritan's Dilemma," refers to the fact that, in providing assistance, the donor also provides a disincentive to the recipient to exert effort to become self-sufficient. The recipient instead becomes dependent on handouts from the donor (Buchanan 1975). The logic of the Samaritan's Dilemma may manifest itself in a number of ways, including, but not limited to, creating disincentives for citizen-recipients to invest in their human capital, start private business ventures, or maintain infrastructure funded by external assistance (Ostrom et al. 2002, 31–32).

A third category of unintended consequences pertains to how foreign intervention can create or escalate conflict. One of the most important studies in this area was carried out by Terry (2002), who points out the "paradox of humanitarian action" in conflict-torn areas. Terry notes that interveners tend to react quickly to complex emergencies without thinking of the political and ethical consequences of their actions. The resulting paradox is that, while many foreign interventions are aimed at removing human suffering, the neglect of the broader effects often leads to a perpetuation and escalation of conflict, which in turn contributes to the very suffering the interventions purport to alleviate. In a series of case studies of Pakistan, Honduras, Thailand, and Zaire, Terry demonstrates in gruesome detail how the rush by outsiders to "do something" often results in resources ending up in the hands of combatants who are among the main contributors to human suffering in the first place.

Other studies reinforce this point. Nunn and Qian (2014) analyze the effect of US food aid on conflict in recipient countries and find that, on average, US food aid increases the incidence of civil war both in terms of the probability of the onset of conflict and the duration of conflict. They explain this finding by highlighting the role of "aid stealing," which refers to armed groups funding conflict through expropriated aid provided by outsiders with the intention of assisting those in need.

A final category of unintended consequences includes crimes perpetuated by interveners against the citizens they purport to assist. Past reported crimes by interveners vary and include assault, fraud, smuggling, theft, and torture (see Casert 1997). Among the most disturbing crimes are the sexual exploitation and abuse of women and children which has been well documented in the case of UN peacekeeping (see Ladley 2005; Defeis 2008; Smith and Miller-de la Cuesta 2010; Smith and Smith 2011; Sieff 2016; Larson 2017).

The type and nature of unintended consequences will vary greatly from case to case. The general point is that interveners face a knowledge problem in anticipating the emergence of these consequences and implementing solutions which avoid creating subsequent negative consequences. This is a central issue in foreign interventions because it is possible for interveners who desire to do good to have the opposite effect.

6.2.4 Knowledge Problems in Executing Operations

Foreign intervention often provides incentives for those being intervened upon to engage in the entrepreneurial search for new ways to avoid or combat the actions of interveners. Interveners face a knowledge problem because people "on the ground" are not passive actors but instead engage in creative discovery to pursue their ends. It is not just a matter of lacking knowledge about local conditions but also that those conditions are dynamic and constantly changing. Interveners may believe they have an effective strategic plan, but as conditions change due to local entrepreneurial responses, so too does the efficacy of that strategy. This dynamic is often most evident in military operations associated with foreign interventions.

For example, Wood (2018) analyzes the effects of substitution in improvised explosive devices (IEDs) by the Afghan and Iraqi insurgencies. Coalition forces were initially unprepared for IEDs and would attach scrap metal and compromised ballistic glass from landfills to their vehicles for any extra degree of protection (ABC News 2004). Billions of dollars were spent on creating and updating counter-IED technologies and techniques. Despite this effort, the number of effective IED incidents grew uninterrupted and dramatically over the course of the war in Afghanistan between 2002 and 2010, and in Iraq between 2003 and the growing impact of the Sunni Awakening in 2007 (Allison et al. 2010; Cordsman et al. 2010).

The reason is that the insurgency responded to changes in US military strategy by changing their methods and techniques for developing and deploying IEDs against occupiers. For example, in 2007 the Joint Improvised Explosive Device Defeat Organization (JIEDDO) declared that existing jamming technologies had mostly stopped insurgents from remotely detonating their bombs. But by 2009, this was no longer the case as insurgents had devised new ways to overcome the existing jamming technologies (Higginbotham 2010). Not only had no one planned on IEDs being a problem prior to engaging in these armed interventions, no one had planned on them being a persistent and adaptive problem fueled by the local knowledge substitute weapon inputs.

The broader issue is this. Planners must design a strategy when intervening in a foreign society. Those being intervened upon, however, are not passive actors. Instead, they will adapt and respond to the strategy of the interveners. Due to uncertainty in an open-ended system, planners cannot entirely foresee how those being intervened upon will respond. This limited knowledge can limit the effectiveness of operations absent adaptability on part of interveners. This adaptability, in turn, is a function of the political institutions governing the intervention.

6.3   Political Economy Problems

Because they are designed and implemented by governments, foreign interventions are fundamentally political in nature. Politics, both within the intervening country as well as in the society being intervened upon, shape and influence what is feasible. Political factors also influence the adaptability of interveners in the face of the various knowledge problems discussed in the previous section. There are four categories of political economy issues that are relevant for foreign interventions.

6.3.1   The Credible Commitment Problem

In order for reforms to be effective interveners must have the incentive to follow through with the course of action to which they have previously committed. And this incentive must be evident to those living under the reform. This requires finding solutions to the credible commitment problem which can be understood as follows. Without a binding and credible commitment to engaging in a specific course of action, those involved in foreign interventions may have an incentive to renege on the announced course of action in future periods (see Coyne 2008a; Coyne and Boettke 2009; Flores and Nooruddin 2009; Coyne and Pellillo 2011).

For example, if citizens expect that interveners will capriciously change their policies in future periods, then they will not believe announcements made in the present. These types of credible commitment problems have hindered efforts in Afghanistan where constant changes to policy by interveners have led to fundamental and widespread uncertainty on the part of Afghan leaders and citizens. As Stewart (2010, n.p.) explains,

> We [the United States and its allies] armed militias in 2001, disarmed them through a demobilization program in 2003, and rearmed them again in 2006 as community defense forces. We allowed local autonomy in 2001, pushed for a strong central government in 2003, and returned to decentralization in 2006. First we tolerated opium crops; then we proposed to eradicate them through aerial spraying; now we expect to live with opium production for decades.

This lack of commitment to a particular policy can hinder the credibility of interveners while contributing to regime uncertainty, which refers to instability in the rules of the game. Returning again to Afghanistan, Stewart (2010, n.p.) explains, "[f]rustrated by a lack of progress, the U.S. and its allies have oscillated giddily between contradictory policies. The British government that once championed more generous budgetary support for the Kabul government now portrays it as corrupt, semi-criminal, ineffective, and illegitimate." Such drastic changes in policy imply that both the Afghan government and interveners will be seen as lacking commitment to a particular policy regime making it difficult for citizens to coalesce around reforms.

The credible commitment problem can manifest in other ways during foreign interventions. For example, certain groups may agree to power sharing agreements while occupiers are present, only to later renege once occupiers have exited. In this case, the absence of a credible commitment leads to the unraveling of previous agreements and the potential breakdown of the reconstruction effort.

Solutions to the credible commitment problem require finding ways to credibly signal a commitment to fulfilling promised policies, reforms, and actions while also establishing binding constraints on future behavior. This can be difficult for the reasons discussed earlier regarding the knowledge problems associated with institutional reform (see Sect. 6.2.1, "The Knowledge Problem over Institutions"). Further complicating matters is the subjective perceptions of credibility by those who must live under the reforms (see Coyne and Boettke 2009). For example, if the populace being intervened upon views the interveners as imperial occupiers who seek to impose their will, then it will be difficult for interveners to establish credibility regarding claims of self-determination. Likewise, if there is a long history of violence or hatred between indigenous groups it can be difficult to establish arrangements involving these parties that are viewed as credible by both sides.

6.3.2   The Conflict Between Political and Non-political Goals

Foreign interventions tend to assume that political and non-political—that is, economic, legal, and social—goals are fully compatible with no tradeoff between the desired ends. This view overemphasizes the benefits of democratic political systems and underemphasizes the potential difficulties democracy can create for achieving other goals. While interveners typically develop a comprehensive list of targets and goals to attain related to the establishment of democratic political systems, the reality is that implementation of plans for political reform often undermines other goals (Coyne and Pellillo 2011, 10–12).

Flores and Nooruddin (2009, 5) find that "countries that undergo extensive democratization in the immediate post-conflict period recover more slowly than countries that do not." This may be because "typically early elections in a highly polarized society empower elites, senior military leaders, and organized criminal elements" (US Army 2009, 1–88). Conceptually, this highlights how important the proper consolidation of institutions is for effective post-conflict reforms and recovery. Absent effective constraints, democracy can produce illiberal outcomes—political, economic, social, and legal—that can cause significant harm to the society being intervened upon. Montgomery (2004, 36) captures the potential conflict between political and non-political goals when highlighting the following possible outcomes under foreign intervention: "(1) the rule of law can degenerate into the rule of lawyers—litigious, costly, and dilatory; (2) economic efficiency can turn into profligacy—piratical and predatory; (3) free speech can reward superficiality and extremism; (4) the demand for unfulfilled rights can invite invidious reverse discrimination; (5) checked-and-balanced governmental institutions can yield policy stasis."

These perverse possibilities, of which there are many more, highlight the necessity of establishing effective constraints to ensure that reform efforts result in stable political and economic orders. Yet creating these checks and balances is by no means a simple task, and, as discussed earlier (see Sect. 6.2.1, "The Knowledge Problem over Institutions"), social scientists and practitioners lack the knowledge of how to design effective liberal constitutional rules that will stick over the long run. This is because formal institutions, such as liberal constitutions, must be grounded in informal customs and belief systems, which are largely beyond the reach of policy (Boettke et al. 2008; Coyne 2008a). This places a hard constraint on the ability of interveners to design institutions according to their desires.

6.3.3   Bureaucratic Pathologies

Because foreign interventions are carried out by states, government bureaus play a central role. Scholars have studied the information (Tullock [1965] 2005), incentive (Tullock [1965] 2005; Niskanen 1971, 1975), and epistemic issues (Mises [1944] 1983) facing government bureaus. This literature identifies three patterns of behavior which are relevant to understanding foreign interventions (see Coyne 2008b, 2013; Coyne and Pellillo 2011, 13–15).

First, bureaus involved in foreign interventions will attempt to secure the largest possible share of financial resources and the associated influence over policy related to the intervention. This typically involves agencies investing scarce resources in signaling the relative importance of their bureau over others. It also involves downplaying the relevance of other bureaus involved in the intervention even though that agency may, in reality, be important for overall success.

Second, the competition over scarce resources creates a tension in the design and execution of foreign interventions. Government agencies should be united in the common goals of the intervention yet they are instead competing with one another for funds and control over policy. Each bureau has its own agenda, which may clash with the agendas of other agencies as well as with the overarching goal of what is required for overall success. For example, as Diamond (2005, 28–29) notes, "a number of U.S. government agencies had a variety of visions of how political authority would be reestablished in Iraq. In the bitter, relentless infighting among U.S. government agencies in advance of the war, none of these preferences clearly prevailed."

Third, bureaus will tend to exhaust their entire budgets while continually seeking financial appropriations in order to increase their size and scope. The failure of a bureau to spend its allocated budget typically leads to budget reductions in subsequent periods. This creates the incentive to ensure that budgets are exhausted even if wasteful expenditures are necessary to achieve this outcome. There are four factors that contribute to this bureaucratic waste.

The absence of economic calculation in government agencies (see Sect. 6.2.2, "The Knowledge Problem Within Institutions") means that bureaucrats are unable to gauge the effective allocation, and reallocation, of resources to high-return uses (Mises [1944] 1983). This means that even the most well-intentioned bureaucrats lack access to the economic knowledge to maximize the value of scarce resources. Second, bureaucratic rules tend to be rigid in nature which often prevents flexibility to rapidly changing conditions. This can contribute to the persistence of waste because bureaucrats are limited in their ability to change their behavior due to binding administrative rules. The third factor is the challenge of long information chains, from lower to higher levels, within bureaus (Tullock [1965] 2005; Coyne 2008b, 2013, 115–121). The longer the information chain, the more likely that noise will be introduced into the process of information transmission decreasing the likelihood that bureaucrats at higher levels will receive the necessary information. Fourth, weak lines of accountability provide a disincentive to change behaviors in the face of waste or ineffectiveness.

To provide a concrete example of these dynamics, consider the case of the $544 million "Community Stabilization Program" (CSP) in Iraq which was meant to contribute to economic rebuilding while undermining the insurgency by winning the hearts and minds of Iraqi citizens. A 2008 audit by the United States Agency for International Development's (USAID's) Inspector General noted the review was "unable to determine if the Community Stabilization Program was achieving its intended result" while noting that "the audit found evidence of potential fraud occurring in projects." Most disturbingly, the audit found that some funds, which were intended to weaken the insurgency by providing alternative livelihoods to potential recruits, instead went to insurgents and corrupt community leaders (USAID Office of the Inspector General

2008, 8). As this illustrates, bureaucratic pathologies can contribute to undermining the broader goals of foreign interventions.

6.3.4   Self-Interested Elected Officials and Special Interests

Two other political factors influencing the viability of foreign interventions must be taken into account. The first is democratic politics in the intervening country. Elected officials respond to the incentives created by the domestic political institutions within which they act and interact. This creates some predictable behaviors—elected officials will seek policies that benefit their constituency even if they are short-sighted or at odds with the goals of the foreign intervention. This dynamic was evident in the experience of former secretary of defense Robert Gates (2014, n.p.) who recounted that

> I did not just have to wage war in Afghanistan and Iraq and against al Qaeda; I also had to battle the bureaucratic inertia of the Pentagon, surmount internal conflicts within both administrations, avoid the partisan abyss in Congress, evade the single-minded parochial self-interest of so many members of Congress and resist the magnetic pull exercised by the White House, especially in the Obama administration, to bring everything under its control and micromanagement. Over time, the broad dysfunction of today's Washington wore me down, especially as I tried to maintain a public posture of nonpartisan calm, reason and conciliation.

Gates succinctly captures how domestic politics, in conjunction with the political economy of bureaucracy discussed above, can adversely affect foreign interventions.

The second factor is special interests which refer to a collection of individuals who come together to work toward a joint goal. Foreign interventions are typically lavishly funded using taxpayer dollars. The result is that special interests—domestic and foreign, private, public, and non-profit—will actively seek to secure as much funding as possible, as quickly as possible. Special interest groups are problematic because they seek to concentrate benefits on their members while dispersing the associated costs on others. In the context of foreign intervention these "others" may be taxpayers in the intervening county or those living in the society being intervened upon. The result of special interest lobbying is waste and fraud, as well as activities that contribute nothing to accomplishing the goals of the foreign intervention.

To understand how special interests can influence foreign interventions, consider that the US military sector incentivizes unproductive entrepreneurship—entrepreneurship that is zero-sum and wealth-destroying—during times of peace as special interests seek to secure portions of the military budget (Coyne et al. 2016; Coyne and Duncan 2018). The military budget can be seen as a common pool resource, and various private parties seek to influence the gatekeepers to secure as much of the commons as possible for their own benefit at the expense of taxpayers (see Coyne and Duncan 2018).

These tendencies are intensified during foreign interventions due to an injection of significant funds along with highly imperfect monitoring and accountability processes (Coyne et al. 2016). These realities are well documented in both Afghanistan and Iraq (see Commission on Wartime Contracting in Iraq and Afghanistan 2011) as well as in numerous other foreign interventions (see Coyne 2008a, 2013). Successful special interests internalize the benefits of their actions while dispersing a significant portion of the associated costs onto others. This can undermine foreign interventions by diverting resources and effort toward negative-sum activities that contribute nothing to achieving the desired goals.

6.4   Conclusion

Foreign intervention is viewed by many as a viable top-down solution to addressing a variety of actual and potential crises around the world. We have highlighted an array of constraints facing interveners. Interveners suffer from several variations of the knowledge problem which limits their ability to design the world according to ideal plans. These knowledge problems exist independent of any incentive issues involved in foreign interventions. Similarly, interveners face an array of incentive issues which become evident when one considers the political economy of foreign intervention. These political economy issues exist independent of the epistemic problems. In practice, both knowledge and political economy problems co-exist and limit the feasibility of foreign interventions. The implications are as follows.

First, a crucial issue with foreign interventions is their robustness. A robust system is one that generates desirable outcomes in the face of less than ideal conditions (see Boettke and Leeson 2004; Pennington 2011). A fragile system is one that generates undesirable outcomes in the face of imperfect actors. The categories of knowledge and political economy problems considered in this chapter can be used to frame considerations of the robustness of foreign interventions because they illustrate the types of imperfections that face these efforts as well as the undesirable consequences that may emerge. Foreign interventions vary greatly in their purpose, structure, and context. So too does their robustness. Because of this, it is crucial to consider the types of knowledge required for success and whether the appropriate feedback mechanisms and incentives exist so that errors can be corrected to achieve the desired ends.

Second, an appreciation of the knowledge and political economy problems discussed in this chapter indicates that the first-best and often the second- and third-best policies will not be realistic given the knowledge limitations and incentives facing interveners. Therefore, it is important to move away from ideal-type theorizing when considering the outcomes of foreign interventions. Instead, it may be more realistic to consider the worst-case scenario to ensure an appreciation of the potential harms caused by foreign interventions and to consider whether mechanisms exist to avoid or ameliorate those harms.

Finally, the discussion in this chapter emphasizes the importance of focusing on the positive aspects of foreign intervention. Many treatments of foreign intervention focus on the normative aspects of the issue—the moral obligation of governments and what they ought to do to help others. We have emphasized that the positive aspects—what *can* be done—are just as important, if not more important, than the normative aspects of foreign intervention. This is because once one considers the relevant constraints and incentives it may be the case that interveners cannot accomplish the desired normative goals. When this occurs, interventions which at first appear to have significant moral weight actually hold little to no weight whatsoever.

References

ABC News. 2004. Soldiers Must Rely on 'Hillbilly Armor' for Protection. *ABC News*, December 8.

Allison, M., A. Cordsman, and J. Lemieux. 2010. I.E.D. Metrics for Afghanistan January 2004–September 2010. *Center for Strategic and International Studies*, November 11. http://csis-prod.s3.amazonaws.com/s3fs-public/legacy_files/files/publication/100722_ied_iraq_afghan.pdf.

Boettke, P.J. 2001. *Calculation and Coordination: Essays on Socialism and Transitional Political Economy*. London: Routledge.

Boettke, P.J., and P.T. Leeson. 2004. Liberalism, Socialism, and Robust Political Economy. *Journal of Markets and Morality* 7 (1): 99–111.

Boettke, P.J., C.J. Coyne, and P.T. Leeson. 2008. Institutional Stickiness and the New Development Economics. *American Journal of Economics and Sociology* 67 (2): 331–358.

Buchanan, J.M. 1975. The Samaritan's Dilemma. In *Altruism, Morality, and Economic Theory*, ed. E.S. Phelps, 71–85. New York: Russell Sage Foundation.

Casert, R. 1997. U.N. Peacekeepers Accused of Atrocities. *The Seattle Times*, June 25. http://community.seattletimes.nwsource.com/archive/?date=19970625&slug=2546399.

Commission on Wartime Contracting in Iraq and Afghanistan. 2011. *Transforming Wartime Contracting: Controlling Costs, Reducing Risks*. Washington, DC: Commission on Wartime Contracting in Iraq and Afghanistan.

Cordesman, A. J., V. Kocharlakota, and C. Loi. 2010. IED Metrics for Iraq: June 2003–September 2010. *Center for Strategic and International Studies*, November 11. https://csis-prod.s3.amazonaws.com/s3fs-public/legacy_files/files/publication/101110_ied_metrics_combined.pdf.

Coyne, C.J. 2008a. *After War: The Political Economy of Exporting Democracy*. Stanford: Stanford University Press.

———. 2008b. 'The Politics of Bureaucracy' and the Failure of Post-War Reconstruction. *Public Choice* 135 (1/2): 11–22.

———. 2011. The Political Economy of the Creeping Militarization of U.S. Foreign Policy. *Peace Economics, Peace Science and Public Policy* 17 (1): 1–27.

———. 2013. *Doing Bad by Doing Good: Why Humanitarian Action Fails.* Stanford: Stanford University Press.

Coyne, C.J., and P.J. Boettke. 2009. The Problem of Credible Commitment in Reconstruction. *Journal of Institutional Economics* 5 (1): 1–23.

Coyne, C.J., and T.K. Duncan. 2018. The Unproductive Protective State: The U.S. Defense Sector as a Fiscal Commons. In *James M. Buchanan: A Theorist of Political Economy and Social Philosophy*, ed. R.E. Wagner. New York: Palgrave Macmillan Publishers.

Coyne, C.J., and A. Pellillo. 2011. Economic Reconstruction Amidst Conflict: Insights from Afghanistan and Iraq. *Defence and Peace Economics* 22 (6): 627–643.

Coyne, C.J., C. Michaluk, and R. Reese. 2016. Unproductive Entrepreneurship in US Military Contracting. *Journal of Entrepreneurship and Public Policy* 5 (2): 221–239.

Defeis, E.F. 2008. U.N. Peacekeepers and Sexual Abuse and Exploitation: An End to Impunity. *Washington University Global Studies Law Review* 7 (2): 185–214.

Diamond, L. 2005. *Squandered Victory: The American Occupation and the Bungled Effort to Bring Democracy to Iraq.* New York: Henry Holt.

Djankov, S., J.G. Montalvo, and M. Reynal-Querol. 2006. Does Foreign Aid Help? *Cato Journal* 26 (1): 1–28.

Duncan, T.K., and C.J. Coyne. 2015. The Political Economy of Foreign Intervention. In *The Oxford Handbook of Austrian Economics*, ed. P.J. Boettke and C.J. Coyne, 678–697. New York: Oxford University Press.

Flores, T.E., and I. Nooruddin. 2009. Democracy Under the Gun: Understanding Post-Conflict Recovery. *Journal of Conflict Resolution* 53 (1): 3–29.

Gates, R.M. 2009. Balanced Strategy: Reprogramming the Pentagon for a New Age. *Foreign Affairs* 88 (1): 28–40.

Gates, R. M. 2014. The Quiet Fury of Robert Gates. *The Wall Street Journal*, January 7. https://www.wsj.com/articles/no-headline-available-1389128316.

Hayek, F.A. 1945. The Use of Knowledge in Society. *American Economic Review* 35 (4): 519–530.

Higginbotham, A. 2010. U.S. Military Learns to Fight Deadliest Weapons. *Wired*, July 28. https://www.wired.com/2010/07/ff_roadside_bombs/.

Hodler, R. 2007. Rent Seeking and Aid Effectiveness. *International Tax and Public Finance* 14 (5): 525–541.

Knack, S. 2001. Aid Dependence and the Quality of Governance: Cross-Country Empirical Tests. *Southern Economic Journal* 68 (2): 310–329.

Ladley, A. 2005. Peacekeeper Abuse, Immunity and Impunity: The Need for Effective Criminal and Civil Accountability on International Peace Operations. *Politics and Ethics Review* 1 (1): 81–90.

Larson, K. 2017. UN Peacekeepers: Congo Leads World in Sex Abuse Allegations. *Associated Press*, September 22. https://www.apnews.com/abbc13a929264889a110d2bb2cccf01f.

Lavoie, D. 1985a. *Rivalry and Central Planning: The Socialist Calculation Debate Reconsidered.* New York: Cambridge University Press.

———. 1985b. *National Economic Planning: What Is Left?* Washington, DC: Cato Institute.

———. 1986. The Market as a Procedure for Discovery and Conveyance of Inarticulate Knowledge. *Comparative Economic Studies* 28 (Spring): 1–19.

Miesen, M. 2013. The Inadequacy of Donating Medical Devices to Africa. *The Atlantic*, September 20. http://www.theatlantic.com/international/print/2013/09/the-inadequacy-of-donatingmedical-devices-to-africa/279855/.

Mises, L. [1920] 1935. Economic Calculation in the Socialist Commonwealth. In *Collectivist Economic Planning*, ed. F.A. Hayek, 87–130. London: George Routledge & Sons.

———. [1944] 1983. *Bureaucracy.* Indianapolis: Liberty Fund, Inc.

———. [1949] 1996. *Human Action.* 4th ed. Indianapolis: Liberty Fund, Inc.

Montgomery, J.D. 2004. Supporting Postwar Aspirations in Islamic Societies. In *Beyond Reconstruction in Afghanistan: Lessons from Development Experience*, ed. J.D. Montgomery and D.A. Rondinelli, 32–52. New York: Palgrave Macmillan.

Niskanen, W. 1971. *Bureaucracy and Representative Government.* Chicago: Aldine-Atherton.

———. 1975. Bureaucrats and Politicians. *Journal of Law and Economics* 18 (3): 617–643.

Nunn, N., and N. Qian. 2014. U.S. Food Aid and Civil Conflict. *American Economic Review* 104 (6): 1630–1666.

Ostrom, E.C., C. Gibson, S. Shivakumar, and K. Andersson. 2002. *Aid, Incentives, and Sustainability.* Stockholm: Swedish International Development Cooperation Agency.

Pennington, M. 2011. *Robust Political Economy: Classical Liberalism and the Future of Public Policy*. Cheltenham: Edward Elgar Publishing, Ltd.

Pritchett, L., and M. Woolcock. 2004. Solutions When the Solution Is the Problem: Arraying the Disarray in Development. *World Development* 32 (2): 191–212.

Shin, D.C. 1994. On the Third Wave of Democratization: A Synthesis and Evaluation of Recent Theory and Research. *World Politics* 47 (1): 135–170.

Sieff, K. 2016. Members of a U.N. Peacekeeping Force in the Central African Republic Allegedly Turned to Sexual Predation, Betraying Their Duty to Protect. *The Washington Post*, February 27. http://www.washingtonpost.com/sf/world/2016/02/27/peacekeepers/?utm_term=.11be9d979aa2.

Smith, C.A., and M. Miller-de la Cuesta. 2010. Human Trafficking in Conflict Zones: The Role of Peacekeepers in the Formation of Networks. *Human Rights Review* 12 (3): 287–299.

Smith, C.A., and H. Smith. 2011. Human Trafficking: The Unintended Effects of United Nations Interventions. *International Political Science Review* 32 (2): 125–145.

Stewart, R. 2010. Afghanistan: What Could Work. *The New York Review of Books*, January 14. http://www.nybooks.com/articles/2010/01/14/afghanistan-what-could-work/.

Svensson, J. 2000. Foreign Aid and Rent-Seeking. *Journal of International Economics* 51 (2): 437–446.

Terry, F. 2002. *Condemned to Repeat? The Paradox of Humanitarian Action*. Ithaca: Cornell University Press.

Tullock, G. [1965] 2005. *Bureaucracy*. Indianapolis: Liberty Fund, Inc.

US Army. 2009. *The U.S. Army Stability Operations Field Manual: U.S. Army Field Manual No. 3-07*. Ann Arbor: The University of Michigan Press.

USAID Office of the Inspector General. 2008. *Audit of USAID/Iraq's Community Stabilization Program Audit Report No. E-267-08-001-P*. Washington, DC: USAID Office of the Inspector General. https://oig.usaid.gov/sites/default/files/audit-reports/e-267-08-001-p.pdf.

Wood, G. 2018. The Enemy Votes: Bargaining Failure and Weapons Improvisation. *Economics of Peace and Security Journal* 13 (1): 25–32.

7

When Is Top-Down State-Building Appropriate?

Jennifer Murtazashvili and Ilia Murtazashvili

7.1 Introduction

The end of the Cold War suggested an end to the ideological debates over capitalism and communism. Despite this, political order and economic development have proven elusive. State fragility remains an important reality in much of the world. The response has typically been costly state-building efforts. These efforts involve massive investments by the international community to establish central government capacity (Ghani and Lockhart 2009). They are often referred to as "liberal peacebuilding" because of their focus on establishing a democratic state, usually via holding elections for national office. The presumption of these efforts is that a

We thank Virgil Henry Storr and Stefanie Haeffele, and the participants in the Hayek Program Responding to Crisis Symposium at the Mercatus Center at George Mason University, for exceptionally useful comments.

J. Murtazashvili (✉) • I. Murtazashvili
Graduate School of Public and International Affairs, University of Pittsburgh, Pittsburgh, PA, USA
e-mail: jmurtaz@pitt.edu; ilia.murtazashvili@pitt.edu

© The Author(s) 2020
S. Haeffele, V. H. Storr (eds.), *Government Responses to Crisis*, Mercatus Studies in Political and Social Economy, https://doi.org/10.1007/978-3-030-39309-0_7

stronger national government, along with national elections, will contribute to political stability, as well as economic development.

The economics of anarchy suggests that such top-down approaches can be misguided. This approach emphasizes that the state does not have a monopoly on good order and working relations (Powell and Stringham 2009). This is especially the case with weak states, where by necessity people often rely on communities because they cannot rely on the state. In some situations, individuals may experience improved human development outcomes after the state fails (Leeson 2007b). Nor do communities simply accept the government predation. Rather, like any prey, they seek to actively evade the state (Vahabi 2015, 2016).

State-building efforts usually presume that communities are incapable of governance, or that their space is ungoverned. Such presumptions can create conflict during state-building processes between organizations that are locally legitimate and new ones supported by the international community. Yet self-governing communities also face challenges that benefit from centralized intervention in community affairs. In addition, it is important to keep in mind that a government response in some circumstances results in pro-poor outcomes (Akaateba et al. 2018).

Recognition of the ability to self-govern, but also the importance of state intervention, suggests that the challenge of state-building is one of diagnosis. The diagnostic approach that we have in mind involves first identifying what works locally as far as self-governance is concerned (Ostrom 2007). Such diagnosis will provide insight into two situations. The first is when communities are unable to provide public goods because they transcend boundaries of several communities or are costly to provide. In each case, self-governance may be operating locally, but it cannot achieve economies of scale in the provision of public goods. The second situation is where self-governance has broken down, in which case the international community may have an opportunity to help establish local governance institutions.

We illustrate the limitations based on original qualitative evidence collected in Afghanistan. Our analysis is based in part on findings from fieldwork. In this regard, we owe a debt to Ostrom (1990), who used fieldwork to understand the important divide between de jure and de facto governing institutions. Indeed, one of the main contributions of the Bloomington School of institutional analysis is the importance of fieldwork (Aligica 2017; Boettke et al. 2013). Substantively, customary self-governing organizations provide a wide range of public goods in rural Afghanistan, but such organizations are not a panacea. Security considerations can often overwhelm villages. In the post-2001 context, the most prominent security challenge comes from Taliban and ISIS-affiliated insurgents, although in the past, the government has often been a source of instability of village governance. Villages are also constrained in their ability to build costly public goods. An example is a road, which is critical to reducing the costs of participating in markets but is challenging to provide under conditions of anarchy. Another challenge that villages may not be able to address is that roads require security, which is a persistent challenge. Yet we also find that community governance is generally resilient despite state fragility, which suggests that international efforts to establish local governance in the countryside, including through the World Bank's National Solidarity Program, may have diverted resources from more productive uses.

Such diagnosis of what communities can and cannot do is important to understanding where government is necessary in what is overall a rural society where custom has more weight in people's daily lives than the state's parchment rules. Yet it is important to keep in mind that our diagnostic approach, while providing insight into a role for government, still very much suggests an approach that helps constrain the power of government officials. The Afghan state remains highly centralized. These formal political institutions conflict with de facto political institutions, which are polycentric. A more productive strategy involves institutional layering, whereby state-building proceeds with a clearer understanding of what works and what does not work, with the goal of layering formal institutions upon informal ones that are proven effective, as well as in filling governance gaps based on concrete evidence of the breakdown of community governance structures.

7.2 Better off Stateless?

Post-conflict reconstruction is often a top-down process. The goal is to construct a more competent state. The economic justification for doing so is that the state is able to achieve economies of scale in public goods provision, such as the provision of security and protection of property rights (North 1981; Tilly 1990). The state is viewed as instrumental to political order and economic development, which are also interrelated: economic development provides the foundation for revenue that the state can then use to establish order internally, but also to defend its borders from external adversaries.

Olson (1993) argued that stability increased the chances that the state, which he referred to as a stationary bandit, provides public goods. However, when some in an organization have more power than others, they may use it to expropriate property (Leeson 2007a; Weingast 1995). Indeed, the state is often the fundamental source of underdevelopment in many contexts (Bates 1981; Scott 1999). Like most things in economics and political economy, whether the state does what is in the interest of society depends on institutions. The state is only expected to improve economic development when political institutions constrain arbitrary exercise of power and when political institutions are inclusive (Bates 2017; North et al. 2009). Constraints on the government are necessary for the state to commit credibly to protecting property rights. In post-conflict settings, the state may be unable to do so, which undermines the effectiveness of post-conflict reconstruction efforts (Coyne and Boettke 2009). In addition, it is important that the state has information about which policies increase economic development. Polycentric political institutions are important in this regard. Political decentralization may also constrain the state (Mokyr 1990; Myerson 2014). Thus, polycentric governance is a source of both information and constraints that improve development prospects.

The literature above suggests that in some situations, namely when there exists political power, but political institutions provide few constraints on rulers, predation will prevail. The economics of anarchy literature suggests that in such situations, state failure may make society better off. In these studies, anarchy is defined as the absence of state control of economic, political, and social affairs (Leeson 2006). The anarchy literature recognizes that many organizations are capable of providing public goods, not just the state (Leeson 2014; Skarbek 2014; Stringham 2015).

Leeson (2007b) explicitly argues that under certain conditions, state failure may make society better off. First, as noted above, there is nothing that ensures government will promote economic development. Hence, communities may be victims of government transgressions of their presumptive rights prior to state collapse. Second, self-governance often works well in such contexts. Customary and tribal institutions are often a reliable source of governance (Baldwin 2013). Thus, state collapse sometimes improves society's wellbeing, such as Somalia. Similarly, Scott (2009, 2012) finds that anarchy is often a socially beneficial response to state predation. Individuals and organizations may even supply economic institutions, including private property, when the government is unwilling to do so (Leeson and Boettke 2009). Importantly, such protective entrepreneurs have market incentives to carry out on their promise of protecting property, whereas the state may have few such incentives.

7.3 Why Government?

There are few reasons to question the argument that statelessness is sometimes better than a predatory state. There is also some good evidence that in places like Somalia, state collapse improved wellbeing in some communities (Powell et al. 2008). It is also reasonable to contend that the presence of self-governing institutions also provides a foundation for post-conflict reconstruction. To be sure, customary and tribal organizations may in some cases be corrupt or captured (Acemoglu et al. 2014; Palagashvili 2018). Yet it is just as clear that in many instances, self-governance can provide many public goods. In such instances, the development community can partner with preexisting institutions to figure out what communities need, how to most efficiently implement aid policies, and to develop a more robust civil society.

The anarchy literature does not assume that society ought to remain stateless. Rather, it considers under what conditions the rise of the state could be justified from an efficiency perspective. Thus, if we accept that states are often predatory, and self-governing organizations can be effective in providing public goods, then the next question is when government intervention in community affairs might make these same communities better off.

There are at least two situations when a greater government presence may be appropriate for communities in a fragile state. The first is for public goods whose benefits transcend several communities or that are costly to provide. Some public goods benefit and require the participation of several communities. This requires coordination across communities, which may be challenging in the absence of government. In contrast, when the benefits from a public good affect only a single community, it is less likely that the government will be needed to provide them.

Security and roads are two examples whose benefits transcend communities and that may be costly to provide. Security is an important example of a public good. In some situations, security may be provided without the state. However, it is challenging to provide, and many communities may simply be unable to respond to threats posed by insurgencies. This does not mean communities are irrelevant. Their participation is often critical in fighting insurgencies. Roads are another example. Building roads may be both costly and require many communities to participate. In addition, the roads often require security, which is often lacking in collapsed states. In such situations, communities still may provide a key role in production of goods or services (e.g., Olken 2007), but they must do so in partnership with government or the international community.

The second situation in which government may be necessary is when self-governance has broken down or is predatory. Communities vary in the extent to which they provide a framework for governance (Agrawal and Gibson 1999). When informal powerholders are unconstrained, they can behave like an extractive state (Acemoglu et al. 2014). There may also be biases of traditional decision-making, such as the exclusion of women from collective decision-making, or choosing projects that benefit men more than women and children (Beath et al. 2013; Olken 2010; Tripp 1997). Another is that self-governance no longer lacks cohesion, such as by out-migration or social changes that undermine social capital within a community (Ostrom 2005).

These situations suggest a positive role for government in state-building. However, they are also based on diagnosing the competencies of local self-governance. A diagnostic approach to state-building is necessary to limit the role of government in state-building. Large influxes of aid money can result in additional corruption that makes political institutions more extractive (Dutta et al. 2013; Leeson and Skarbek 2009). The humanitarians may also be a source of bad behavior, as they are often unconstrained by domestic legal rules and unaccountable to rules abroad (Coyne 2013). A more promising approach is to identify what works locally, and then to use that information to justify government intervention. Even where there are limits to communities, the response should also be layered in the sense that state-building proceeds through partnerships with government, communities, and international donors.

7.4 Reconstructing Afghanistan

7.4.1 Afghanistan: Better off Stateless?

Afghanistan has robust customary institutions that transcend ethnic groups. One of the main differences between tribal and customary institutions is that the former is based on ethnicity, while the latter are social institutions that are generally tied to community. Pashtunwali, the Pashtun tribal code, is an example of an informal institution governing behavior that has its basis in ethnicity. Although analysts of Afghanistan often emphasize the strength of tribal ties (e.g., Rubin 2002), the organization of Afghan villages is rooted in custom rather than tribe (J. Murtazashvili 2016b). Communities are usually organized around three customary organizations: a village representative (maliks, qaryadars, arbabs, wakils, etc.), deliberative councils (shura or jirga), and religious authorities (mullahs). The village representative is the first among equals. He is not a chief and does not have a formal office. Rather, maliks usually hold their position because they are respected in the community. The shura is a deliberative council. Although it does not include women, it provides a forum that brings together men in the village to discuss matters of collective importance. A shura can also bring together people from several communities. Mullahs are typically self-trained. They are the lowest level of Islamic authority in Afghanistan, but participate in village governance, including addressing inheritance disputes, which often involve matters of Islamic law (J. Murtazashvili 2016b).

Customary authorities have always had a significant role in Afghan politics. During two wars with the British during the nineteenth century, the wars were fought by mainly tribal levies (Johnson 2012). The state has also never extended far beyond traditional strongholds, such as Kandahar and Kabul, which meant that self-governance was the norm in many parts of the country.

Despite the importance of customary institutions, the Afghan government has generally had little patience for them. Although tribal leaders came together in 1747 to form Afghanistan, the early Afghan state was a confederation of loosely connected groups. Rulers subsequently viewed the decentralized state as a source of disorder. For much of the next century and a half, after the Afghan state was formed, there was an uneasy balance between state and informal powerholders. This changed when Abdur Rahman, the king from 1880 to 1901, waged wars of internal colonization to defeat what he called the "middlemen" of Afghan society, including customary and tribal powerbrokers. Even though he consolidated power, Abdur Rahman wanted to keep people poor, and so he destroyed property rights (I. Murtazashvili and J. Murtazashvili 2016b).

From 1919 to 1929, Amanullah—Abdur Rahman's grandson—proposed many reforms, including the creation of legal private property, schooling for girls, and abolition of the bride price. Such reforms promised to improve prospects for economic development. However, the pace of reforms was rapid, which provoked resistance from tribal society (Poullada 1973). He was eventually overthrown after a brief civil war. He was a liberal reformer compared to his grandfather, but Amanullah also had little patience for tribal and customary institutions, which he viewed as a source of economic underdevelopment. Amanullah attempted to replace these informal rules and procedures with legal ones, such as by recognizing only legal property, rather than customary property, and legal decisions of courts, rather than customary or tribal adjudication. The disregard of customary governance provoked a resistance movement. Although he was able to defeat several challenges to his rule, he was eventually ousted by a small army led by a Tajik warrior from the North of

Kabul. The Tajik, Kalakani, did not last long himself, as he fell to the army of Nadir Shah, who was formerly one of Amanullah's generals. Nadir Shah was the first of the dynasty known as the Musahiban, whose rule was characterized by maintaining the status quo. There were fewer concerted efforts to challenge Afghan social norms and institutions. There was also no economic development to speak of, which contributed to the rise of the Afghan community party. The communists came to power when the Khalq, the radical faction of Afghanistan's communist party, the People's Democratic Party of Afghanistan (PDPA), staged a palace coup in April 1978. The Khalq government believed that tribal and customary institutions were oppressive and socially inefficient, which led them to replace customary representatives with their own operatives. During this time, many customary leaders were removed from power, killed, or disappeared.

By 1979, the country had descended into civil war. The communist reforms, including land expropriation, were met with resistance. The Soviets invaded in 1979 to slow the pace of reform, but by that time, mujahideen—holy warriors—had organized against the Afghan communists and their Soviet allies. The Taliban emerged but fled to Pakistan. From 1979 to 1992, the PDPA remained the government, although conflict and violence led to the collapse of the Afghan state. By 1996, the Taliban controlled much of the country, which they did until 2001, when the US invaded.[1] One of the consequences of civil war was the collapse of the Afghan state. Was the country better off after state collapse? A case could certainly be made that the predatory Afghan state made life worse for Afghans than when it collapsed. We also know that customary governance remains an important source of governance in Afghanistan. According to fieldwork conducted in over thirty villages, J. Murtazashvili (2016b) found that self-governance was resilient. After decades of war, customary governance reasserted itself.

One of the findings from this fieldwork is that Afghans are often able to manage affairs within villages quite well. They can resolve conflicts arising within villages much more effectively than if they sought out courts. This includes land conflicts, where the state is often unreliable. Self-governance of land relations typically results in effective land governance (I. Murtazashvili and J. Murtazashvili 2015, 2016a). Communities are also able to provide public goods, such as the management of water resources and regulation of forests, within the village, or across a small handful of villages.

7.4.2   Where Government May Do Some Good

Another feature of the Afghan context, besides robust community governance, is that the country is extremely poor. To say that a country is better off stateless does not mean development will occur once the state fails. There is a role for top-down state-building in Afghanistan to improve development prospects. However, fieldwork is necessary to understand where such intervention is socially beneficial. It showed several areas where there was a desire for a top-down response. First, communities were not able to provide certain types of public goods. Security is one of them. There were many accounts from villagers about the brutality of the Taliban and militias, and the return of the Taliban was something that many villagers feared.

Although communities can often solve land disputes themselves, there are also larger-scale conflicts in many parts of the country between rival groups competing for the same land. These are different than intra-village disputes. An example is the land situation in Garmser, where large numbers of people have claims to land but do not feel they have access to courts to resolve those disputes, nor do customary institutions provide a solution (Baczko 2016). In Garmser, the Taliban helped resolve land conflicts. This is a top-down solution because communities cannot impose order, and so they rely on an insurgent organization (a third party) to resolve disputes. There are also conflicts between nomad and settled communities that often tax the ability of communities to resolve conflicts (Stanfield et al. 2010). Often, the government is called upon to help alleviate conflict that arises when nomads return to areas and claim priority rights to land.

There is also the more general challenge of defending communities against the Taliban. The Taliban, when they come to a village, can often overwhelm it. In those communities, the US military can improve security. In some contexts, US military presence leads to violence and conflict that undermines liberty (Coyne and Hall Blanco 2016). Although security intervention can have features of a public bad, informants during fieldwork often expressed support for the US intervention in Afghanistan. They viewed security as something that they could not provide themselves.

Public goods that transcended the boundaries of communities, especially roads, also presented challenges for self-governing communities. Villages are often able to provide some types of public goods, such as resolving disputes within their community. They might also be able to provide a water manager to look after the irrigation canals. But for something like a road, they required more help from the government and international community. In addition, there is the challenge of securing the road once it is built, which may require some sort of armed presence that a single village or even a couple of villages may not be able to provide.

Another challenge is that in some communities, self-governance was ineffective or had become predatory. In some communities, strongmen returned to communities to take advantage of foreign aid money coming into villages. In those villages, respondents complained that they were facing a type of extortion. In some communities, the challenge was that people were displaced during times of violence and faced challenges in reconstituting their system of customary governance. Yet it is important to keep in mind that most communities exhibited substantial resilience. After violence subsided, many returned to their community, and they together reconstituted and updated customary methods of governance.

There are several caveats that are in order. The fieldwork from Afghanistan provides insight into a potential role for government. Of course, there remains a challenge of implementation, which is really a challenge of overcoming incentive problems that come with foreign aid and development assistance. Historically, Afghanistan has been a rentier state. The British, then the Soviets, and today the Americans provide the government with most of its revenue. In the current context, foreign aid has even destabilized village governance. In some communities, commanders returned because they wanted some of the money from international agencies. More generally, it is not clear that aid is tailored to the areas where the state is necessary.

Another is that initiatives to establish local governance may not be good fits with local customary institutions. One of the goals of the National Solidarity Program (NSP), which was funded by the World Bank, sought to establish village governance by creating Community Development Councils (CDCs) in tens of thousands of villages.[2] The CDCs would come with around $60,000 USD to promote development—a substantial sum in Afghanistan. These are standard community-driven development projects, which are common in developing countries (King and Samii 2014). Yet they are not necessarily an improvement in village governance. The reason is that in many instances, there is already customary governance in place. Indeed, in some contexts, governance quality was undermined by NSP projects (Beath et al. 2015).

The international community also reinforces inefficient power structures. The old, centralized bureaucratic institutions were not entirely destroyed during conflict. They often provide a path of least resistance with which the international community can easily partner. International assistance helped reinforce, rather than transform dysfunctional bureaucratic structures and excessively centralized formal governance. A result is that citizens have not experienced meaningful changes in the way government exercises its authority (J. Murtazashvili 2016a).

One way to deal with these challenges is to work with self-governing institutions. This requires overcoming the bias against them, which is that such institutions are backward or hierarchical. They provide public goods and are somewhat inclusive. Yet the Afghan state as constructed is highly centralized. A result is that there remains little opportunity for institutional layering, at least at the formal level. There is some degree of informal power-sharing, but formal rules have been slow to adapt.

7.5 Conclusion

Post-conflict reconstruction is a response to large-scale crises. Unlike crises arising from natural disasters in contexts like the US, which have the advantage of political stability and private property rights, state collapse results in a breakdown of political institutions, weak private property rights, and in some locales, a weakening of the ties that tie together communities. These challenges are one of the reasons why there is often a preference for large-scale, top-down efforts to reconstruct states. Those programs, whose costs run into the trillions of dollars, seek to construct a more powerful state to improve prospects for political order and economic development.

Such top-down perspectives on state-building are overly ambitious and often poorly designed. They understate the importance of self-governance in such contexts, as well as the challenges that arise from efforts to build a failed state, such as how large increases in foreign aid can result in corruption and reinforces existing inefficient institutions. Self-governance is often what works in such contexts.

Yet it is important to not eliminate a role for government in such contexts. There are limits to anarchy, such as when public goods are costly or transcend many communities. Self-governance may also be predatory, or it may simply not be as effective as it had been before, perhaps due to out-migration because of war and violence. There are also options for use of soft power, or winning hearts and minds through education, rather than conventional security (Aldrich 2014). Such state-building proceeds by acknowledging a role for self-governance, identifying through community consultation what development policies the communities believe will improve their opportunities, shifting the priority from constructing a democratic state to constructing a limited government, and more closely fitting formal political institutions to what is often a de facto polycentric structure of governance.

Notes

1. Edwards (2002) provides a compelling account of the link between the community government and the rise of the Afghan Taliban.
2. Depending on the source, Afghanistan has between 20,000 and 40,000 villages, most with no more than a few hundred people. The total population is less than 25 million.

References

Acemoglu, D., T. Reed, and J.A. Robinson. 2014. Chiefs: Economic Development and Elite Control of Civil Society in Sierra Leone. *Journal of Political Economy* 122 (2): 319–368.

Agrawal, A., and C.C. Gibson. 1999. Enchantment and Disenchantment: The Role of Community in Natural Resource Conservation. *World Development* 27 (4): 629–649.

Akaateba, M.A., H. Huang, and E.A. Adumpo. 2018. Between Co-production and Institutional Hybridity in Land Delivery: Insights from Local Planning Practice in Peri-Urban Tamale, Ghana. *Land Use Policy* 72: 215–226.

Aldrich, D.P. 2014. First Steps Towards Hearts and Minds? USAID's Countering Violent Extremism Policies in Africa. *Terrorism and Political Violence* 26 (3): 523–546.

Aligica, P.D. 2017. *Institutional Diversity, Pluralism, and Institutional Theory*. New York: Oxford University Press.

Baczko, A. 2016. Legal Rule and Tribal Politics: The US Army and the Taliban in Afghanistan (2001–13). *Development and Change* 47 (6): 1412–1433.

Baldwin, K. 2013. Why Vote with the Chief? Political Connections and Public Goods Provision in Zambia. *American Journal of Political Science* 57 (4): 794–809.

Bates, R.H. 1981. *Markets and States in Tropical Africa: The Political Basis of Agricultural Policies: With a New Preface*. Berkeley, CA: University of California Press.

———. 2017. *The Development Dilemma: Security, Prosperity, and a Return to History*. Princeton: Princeton University Press.

Beath, A., F. Christia, and R. Enikolopov. 2013. Empowering Women: Evidence from a Field Experiment in Afghanistan. *American Political Science Review* 107 (3): 540–557.

———. 2015. The National Solidarity Programme: Assessing the Effects of Community-Driven Development in Afghanistan. *International Peacekeeping* 22 (4): 302–320.

Boettke, P.J., L. Palagashvili, and J. Lemke. 2013. Riding in Cars with Boys: Elinor Ostrom's Adventures with the Police. *Journal of Institutional Economics* 9 (4): 407–425.

Coyne, C.J. 2013. *Doing Bad by Doing Good: Why Humanitarian Action Fails*. Palo Alto, CA: Stanford University Press.

Coyne, C.J., and P.J. Boettke. 2009. The Problem of Credible Commitment in Reconstruction. *Journal of Institutional Economics* 5 (1): 1–23.

Coyne, C.J., and A.R. Hall Blanco. 2016. Empire State of Mind: The Illiberal Foundations of Liberal Hegemony. *The Independent Review* 21 (2): 237.

Dutta, N., P.T. Leeson, and C.R. Williamson. 2013. The Amplification Effect: Foreign Aid's Impact on Political Institutions. *Kyklos* 66 (2): 208–228.

Edwards, D.B. 2002. *Before Taliban: Genealogies of the Afghan Jihad*. Berkeley, CA: University of California Press.

Ghani, A., and C. Lockhart. 2009. *Fixing Failed States: A Framework for Rebuilding a Fractured World*. New York: Oxford University Press.

Johnson, R. 2012. *The Afghan Way of War: How and Why They Fight*. New York: Oxford University Press.

King, E., and C. Samii. 2014. Fast-Track Institution Building in Conflict-Affected Countries? Insights from Recent Field Experiments. *World Development* 64: 740–754.

Leeson, P.T. 2006. Efficient Anarchy. *Public Choice* 130 (1–2): 41–53.

———. 2007a. Anarchy, Monopoly, and Predation. *Journal of Institutional and Theoretical Economics* 163 (3): 467–482.

———. 2007b. Better Off Stateless: Somalia Before and After Government Collapse. *Journal of Comparative Economics* 35 (4): 689–710.

———. 2014. *Anarchy Unbound: Why Self-Governance Works Better than You Think*. New York: Cambridge University Press.

Leeson, P.T., and P.J. Boettke. 2009. Two-Tiered Entrepreneurship and Economic Development. *International Review of Law and Economics* 29 (3): 252–259.

Leeson, P.T., and D. Skarbek. 2009. What Can Aid Do? *Cato Journal* 29 (3): 391–397.

Mokyr, Joel. 1990. *The Lever of Riches: Technological Creativity and Economic Progress*. Oxford: Oxford University Press.

Murtazashvili, J. 2016a. Afghanistan: A Vicious Cycle of State Failure. *Governance* 29 (2): 163–166.

———. 2016b. *Informal Order and the State in Afghanistan*. New York: Cambridge University Press.

Murtazashvili, I., and J. Murtazashvili. 2015. Anarchy, Self-Governance, and Legal Titling. *Public Choice* 162 (3–4): 287–305.

———. 2016a. The Origins of Property Rights: States or Customary Organizations? *Journal of Institutional Economics* 12 (1): 105–128.

———. 2016b. When Does the Emergence of a Stationary Bandit Lead to Property Insecurity? *Rationality and Society* 28 (3): 335–360.

Myerson, R. 2014. Constitutional Structures for a Strong Democracy: Considerations on the Government of Pakistan. *World Development* 53: 46–54.

North, D.C. 1981. *Structure and Change in Economic History.* New York: W. W. Norton & Company.

North, D.C., J.J. Wallis, and B.R. Weingast. 2009. *Violence and Social Orders: A Conceptual Framework for Interpreting Recorded Human History.* New York: Cambridge University Press.

Olken, B.A. 2007. Monitoring Corruption: Evidence from a Field Experiment in Indonesia. *Journal of Political Economy* 115 (2): 200–249.

———. 2010. Direct Democracy and Local Public Goods: Evidence from a Field Experiment in Indonesia. *American Political Science Review* 104 (2): 243–267.

Olson, M. 1993. Dictatorship, Democracy, and Development. *American Political Science Review* 87 (3): 567–576.

Ostrom, E. 1990. *Governing the Commons: The Evolution of Institutions for Collective Action.* New York: Cambridge University Press.

———. 2005. *Understanding Institutional Diversity.* Princeton: Princeton University Press.

———. 2007. A Diagnostic Approach for Going Beyond Panaceas. *Proceedings of the National Academy of Sciences of the United States of America* 104 (39): 15181–15187.

Palagashvili, L. 2018. African Chiefs: Comparative Governance Under Colonial Rule. *Public Choice* 174 (3–4): 277–300.

Poullada, L.B. 1973. *Reform and Rebellion in Afghanistan, 1919–1929; King Amanullah's Failure to Modernize a Tribal Society.* Ithaca: Cornell University Press.

Powell, B., and E.P. Stringham. 2009. Public Choice and the Economic Analysis of Anarchy: A Survey. *Public Choice* 140 (3–4): 503–538.

Powell, B., R. Ford, and A. Nowrasteh. 2008. Somalia After State Collapse: Chaos or Improvement? *Journal of Economic Behavior & Organization* 67 (3–4): 657–670.

Rubin, B.R. 2002. *The Fragmentation of Afghanistan: State Formation and Collapse in the International System.* New Haven, CT: Yale University Press.

Scott, J.C. 1999. *Seeing Like a State: How Certain Schemes to Improve the Human Condition Have Failed.* New Haven, CT: Yale University Press.

————. 2009. *The Art of Not Being Governed: An Anarchist History of Upland Southeast Asia.* New Haven, CT: Yale University Press.

————. 2012. *Two Cheers for Anarchism: Six Easy Pieces on Autonomy, Dignity, and Meaningful Work and Play.* Princeton: Princeton University Press.

Skarbek, D. 2014. *The Social Order of the Underworld: How Prison Gangs Govern the American Penal System.* New York: Oxford University Press.

Stanfield, J.D., Y. Safar, A. Salam, and J. Brick. 2010. Rangeland Administration in (Post) Conflict Conditions: The Case of Afghanistan. In *Innovations in Land Rights: Recognition, Administration and Governance*, ed. K. Deininger, C. Augustinus, S. Enmark, and P. Munro-Faure, 300–317. Washington, DC: World Bank.

Stringham, E.P. 2015. *Private Governance: Creating Order in Economic and Social Life.* New York: Oxford University Press.

Tilly, C. 1990. *Coercion Capital and European States A D 990–1990.* Oxford: Blackwell.

Tripp, A.M. 1997. *Changing the Rules: The Politics of Liberalization and the Urban Informal Economy in Tanzania.* Berkeley, CA: University of California Press.

Vahabi, M. 2015. *The Political Economy of Predation: Manhunting and the Economics of Escape.* Cambridge: Cambridge University Press.

————. 2016. A Positive Theory of the Predatory State. *Public Choice* 168 (3–4): 153–175.

Weingast, B.R. 1995. The Economic Role of Political Institutions: Market-Preserving Federalism and Economic Development. *Journal of Law, Economics, and Organization* 11 (1): 1–31.

8

The European Migrant Crisis: A Case Study in Failure of Governmental and Supra-governmental Responses

Paul Dragos Aligica and Thomas Savidge

8.1 Introduction

Some crises are by their very nature international, they cannot be dealt with in their causes and consequences by mere state-level institutions. Externalities, multiple causalities, collective action, and diverse and divergent jurisdictions require the emergence of supra-level arrangements and forms of coordination and organization. One of the main reasons for advocating international political integration and, even more precisely, for the creation of supra-state governance structures complementing and substituting the national states, has been the very problem of crises and crisis management. The European Union (EU) is one of these forms of organization. As such, it offers one of the best case studies of how such

P. D. Aligica (✉)
F. A. Hayek Program for Advanced Study in Philosophy, Politics, and Economics, Mercatus Center at George Mason University, Fairfax, VA, USA
e-mail: paligica@mercatus.gmu.edu

T. Savidge
George Mason University, Fairfax, VA, USA

© The Author(s) 2020
S. Haeffele, V. H. Storr (eds.), *Government Responses to Crisis*, Mercatus Studies in Political and Social Economy, https://doi.org/10.1007/978-3-030-39309-0_8

meta-level structures are handling and coping with international crises. Is the creation of an overarching, supra-national, state-like structure indispensable to solve such problems? Or is a mere coordination mechanism, operating between the existing states, is sufficient? Is a polycentric approach adequate? Or, in fact, is further centralization needed? What could we learn about such dilemmas from the EU and more specifically from particular crises testing the EU and its governance?

This chapter explores the issue through the case of the ongoing migrant crisis. Starting in 2015, the flux of millions of migrants and refugees crossing into Europe has reached a critical point. That generated a sui generis crisis, as the EU countries struggled to cope with a heterogeneous influx of asylum seekers, economic migrants, and even terrorists. Tensions and divisions emerged in the EU over how best to deal with this massive resettlement of people. Taking a look at the case, we get a better sense of the role of the states (and supra-state structures) not only in solving such crises but also in fueling and maintaining them. One could reframe the general questions in more specific ways: when it comes to the migrant crisis, is the current failure of the EU the result of a lack of centralization? Or it is a lack of decentralization and polycentricism? Is it an institutional problem? Or it is a failure to balance and calibrate the governmental responses within a larger and more encompassing governance arrangement, operating above and beyond the separate EU nation states? This chapter will suggest a rather nuanced and perhaps surprising answer.

In a sense, we start from a surprising failure: the EU was supposed to operate at its best precisely in such cases of crisis, as a supra-governmental structure, able to solve the collective action problems generated by situations taking place beyond and between the standard jurisdictions of the national states. Its failure is in many respects stunning. It is tempting to conclude that the institutional structure was not right. But while studying the responses given within the existing structure, it is hard to pinpoint the general institutional arrangement to be blamed for the current situation. The very nature of the problem recommends a solution based on a polycentric system of governance in which different decision centers and administrative units coordinate under an overarching system of rules and coordinating mechanisms. Assuming that such a system was *not* in place, such as system would be on the top of any list of main recommendations as remedies. Yet, the system in place was by all accounts featuring a significant degree of polycentrism. Is then the entire migrant crisis debacle a failure of polycentric governance? A closer look at the concrete facts and developments on the ground—both the problems defining the crisis and the responses to them—will help us determine the answer.

To answer these and related questions, this chapter starts by presenting the basic facts related to the crisis confronting the EU. Then it focuses on the general responses to the crisis. The question of whether this is a crisis due to the polycentric structure of the EU (i.e. resulting from the very institutional design of EU) or a crisis resulting from a botched management of the system is then addressed. The chapter uses the distinction between the structure of a polycentric system and the actions and operations of the decision makers with or within the polycentric system to make the point that such a system cannot work if a polycentric arrangement is run on principles, operational codes, and attitudes that are not consistent with polycentricism. The chapter concludes that this disjunction between structure and decision making is precisely what is happening with the ongoing EU migrant crisis.

8.2 The EU Migrant Crisis

Prior to getting into the issue, we must lay the groundwork for some basic facts and definitions. A 2015 report from the Council on Foreign Relations on Europe's Migration Crisis highlights the distinct labels used, based in international law (Park 2015). An "asylum seeker" is someone fleeing persecution or conflict seeking international protection in accordance with the 1951 Refugee Convention on the Status of Refugees. A "refugee" is an asylum seeker with an approved claim of asylum. On the contrary, an "economic migrant" is someone who leaves his country of origin primarily for personal economic gain. The Council on Foreign Relations report continues by noting that the term "migrant" is a phrase that is used for all three classifications. In its own words, "all refugees are migrants, but not all migrants are refugees" (Park 2015, n.p.). Hence a migrant crisis is to be distinguished from a refugee crisis.

The EU collects data on a variety of topics related to migration. Data are collected annually through the statistical authorities of EU member states and formal reports are produced by Eurostat (the statistical office of the EU). In these datasets, the relevant demographics are broken down into four categories: (1) citizens of a respective country, (2) citizens of another EU country, (3) non-EU citizens, and (4) unknown citizenship (Juchno and Agafitei 2017). Eurostat provides data and reports on all of the above. Yet there are limitations that must be mentioned regarding the data. The data collected covers the entire population of the EU. However, in regard to migrants, certain limitations arise. For example, recently arrived migrants are missing in the sampling frame from each host country, resulting in a lower migrant population size reported than may exist in that country in any given year. In addition, migrants living in "collective households" and "institutions for asylum seekers and migrant workers" are also excluded from the sample, resulting, again, in lower numbers reported. Another issue occurs when migrants do not respond to survey data and specific data collected from households for individuals 16 and over, resulting in lower numbers of migrants reported (Juchno and Agafitei 2017). In spite of these limitations, we are able to estimate the sizable impact migrants have on the EU as well as to get an idea of the large numbers of migrants coming over to the EU.

Our discussion will be primarily concerned with the situation generated by non-EU citizens and unknown citizenship and, as to be described later, the push and pull factors of migrants to come to the EU as well as the role the EU and its member states play in those push and pull factors. Since 2011, there has been a large influx of migrants from North Africa, the Middle East, and Central Asia.

As reported by Eurostat, immigration through legal channels from non-EU countries has varied since 2006. Eurostat reports that roughly between three and four million immigrants enter the EU each year, starting in 2006 all the way through 2014. In 2015, that number increased to about 4.6 million migrants. Much like the snapshot of non-EU citizen population in 2017, a handful of countries have taken in most migrants. Germany, the United Kingdom, France, Spain, and Italy taking in the most migrants while smaller countries such as Estonia, Malta, and Croatia taking in less than 50,000 in 2015 (Juchno and Agafitei 2017, 12).

Table 8.1 Taxonomy of migration factors

Type of migrant	Demand-pull	Supply-push	Network/other
Economic	Labor recruitment	Unemployment or underemployment	Jobs and wage information flow
Non-economic	Family unification	Fleeing war/civil unrest	Communications, transportations, assistance organizations, desire for new experience

Source: Parkins (2010) and Martin and Zurcher (2008)

However, it is important to note again that these numbers do not include the migrants rapidly fleeing war-torn areas seeking asylum.

There is no single factor that brings migrants into the European Union. One could outline the "push" factors (that incentivize migrants to leave their home country) and "pull" factors (that incentivize migrants to come to the EU) and their roles in the current crisis. Parkins (2010) gives an example of such a taxonomy of the factors that affect various types of migration (see Table 8.1).[1]

It is also important to note that push and pull factors are not mutually exclusive. For example, migrants from Libya and Syria have a variety of push and pull factors driving their incentive to come to the EU. Since 2011, there has been an influx in migrants from Libya fleeing the social unrest following the civil war and the collapse of the Gaddafi regime. Recently, thousands of refugees have come from Syria fleeing the civil war. The armed conflicts and civil unrest are obviously push factors. However, factors such greater standard of living, unemployment benefits, and pensions have an important role as pull factors. In addition, Afghans fleeing the Taliban as well as other migrants fleeing poverty and civil unrest in Iraq, Nigeria, Pakistan, Somalia, and Sudan also are incentivized to leave their nation of origin (Park 2015). These are considered push factors affecting the aggregate labor supply of the economies the migrants are entering but also the system of social services, education, and the communities themselves of the EU member states (Zimmerman 1996).

With this recent influx of migrants, the EU and its member states have also contributed to both the push and pull factors of migrants entering the EU in recent years. As noted as early as 1996, major demographic changes were set to affect migration and the EU. Zimmerman (1996, 100) notes six: (1) roughly 80–100 million people will migrate to Europe from less developed regions; (2) expected migration from eastern to western Europe would increase through the early 2000s; (3) western European populations will decline (particularly two percent by 2025 in the EU); (4) total European populations are expected to rise by three percent (with most of this growth coming from Eastern Europe) in the 2000s; (5) countries in North Africa and the Middle East as well as Turkey will grow at a much faster rate than Europe over the same time as Europe's population growth; and (6) western European labor force will age considerably. Much of Zimmerman's predictions came true. However, he did not anticipate the push factors of the conflicts in Libya and Syria and in general the Middle East and North Africa. These greater push factors helped spur an influx in migrants of all types over the past several years.

Another factor Zimmerman failed to note was related to the internal EU structure. In the Schengen area, for instance, 22 EU members (prominently Germany and Sweden) participate where individuals may travel through this area without passport checks.[2] This specific pull factor incentivized many migrants arriving in Greece to travel through the West Balkans attempting to reach the Schengen states, such as Hungary and Slovenia, to get to Germany and Sweden, where they believed they could receive the best welfare benefits (Archick 2016).

These developments have generated significant disruptions and problems at multiple levels for both the population and governance of Europe. The multiple layered system of European governance failed to react as desired. EU-level and state-level tensions as well as tension between states have emerged. Although one may see the problem as a general, aggregated one, impacting a unitary entity called the EU as a whole, the reality is that the impact had different forms, for different European countries. The flexible EU structure (exit, entry, and circulation friendly) amplifies the heterogeneity of the impact. That heterogeneity requires responses and an adjustment process between regions and levels of governance. Again, one may have expected that the EU was structurally prepared for such situations. A look at the EU-level response to the crisis, then a focus on the German approach and its failure, with the ensuing breakdown of cooperation between EU member states, illuminates the magnitude of the systemic failure in the case in point.

8.3 The EU Response

Let us start with the basic observation that the EU's attempts at solving the migrant crisis thus far have been unsuccessful and have even caused significant rifts among member states. While theoretically the capacity to coordinate at the states level via a meta-level structure was supposed to be a strength of the EU, in practice that was illusory. Usually a major point of contention comes over concerns regarding sovereignty. Indeed, in this case, the decision makers at the EU level were unable to navigate the challenge. EU-level authorities attempted to both act unilaterally *and* respect the sovereignty of its member states but ended up disappointing all parties. No solution was reached. The problem got worse. Member states increasingly became concerned over the influx of migrants entering the EU. People responded by becoming aware of the impasse and electing anti-immigrant parties to their respective governments.

Crucial in these developments was the German response, a major veto player—if not the major player—of the EU. In 2015, the EU reported roughly 1.3 million asylum claims, with 476,000 of those claims just for Germany (Greenhill 2016, 26). Angela Merkel gambled on the idea that Germany would inspire other leaders of member states to engage in "European solidarity and burden-sharing" hoping to rally other EU members to support the open-door policy toward migrants (Greenhill 2016, 26). She borrowed the phrase *Wir Schaffen das* (similar to the English "Yes we can") from US President Barack Obama to support her welcoming migrant policy. However, Merkel's hopes were quickly dashed. She did not get the support she was expecting, with political gridlock, emergency defections from the Schengen area, and an overall increase in the number of migrants coming into Germany.

It is noteworthy that Merkel's Germany disregarded the EU's "Dublin regulation"—which deems the first EU country an asylum seeker enters responsible for examining and processing an asylum seeker's application—thus operating openly and illegally outside the EU agreements. The other EU members took offense. Some EU governments came to denounce Germany's open-door policy as unilaterally upending agreed EU asylum procedures and acting in its own agenda regardless of the other member states (Archick 2016, 9). Within Germany itself, public opinion split, with Merkel's Christian Democratic Party rapidly losing favor. In 2015, the Christian Democratic Party lost seats in all three German states while the anti-immigrant Alternative for Germany Party made noteworthy gains (Greenhill 2016, 327). Migration continued to be a major topic in German political life. Merkel's immigration stance continued to lose favor until, in July 2018, Merkel compromised for tighter immigration controls in order to maintain control of the government (Thomas and Marson 2018). Instead of the open-door policy, Merkel advocated for "closed centers" near Germany's borders that would take asylum applications that "would be reviewed quickly" (Thomas and Marson 2018, n.p.). Interior Minister Horst Seehofer, after threatening resignation unless a deal was struck, commented, "We have a clear agreement on how to prevent illegal migration in [the] future on the border between Germany and Austria" (Thomas and Marson 2018, n.p.). It is safe to say that Germany has backed down from its original goals of an open-door policy.

As previously discussed, the lack of coherent policy and Germany's decision to act unilaterally did not bode well with other EU members. It does not even matter whether the intentions were generous and humane in this process. In response to Germany's actions, many parties reacting to the immigrant flux and the turbulences created by it were rapidly growing in strength throughout member states. Poland's Law and Justice Party as well as Hungary's Fidesz Party were bolstered and gained political ground. In addition, Greece and Italy have witnessed the rise of parties that openly confront the pro-emigration stance (Tartar 2017). A key feature of these parties (aside from being anti-immigrant) is their general disdain against the EU. And as these parties gain further political ground, further tensions within the EU and additional national governments resistance to the EU may be expected.

In brief we have seen how the supra-state system failed while at the same time the national states level coordination process which was supposed to bolster, legitimate, and correct the supra-state level, failed as well in egregious ways. The narrative and the basic data are unambiguous in this respect. That being said, we could go beyond this mostly narrative interpretation and illuminate a deeper and more significant aspect and significance of the case.

8.4 Conclusion

As already noted, in many respects this is a surprising failure. The EU was supposed to operate precisely in such cases of crisis as a supra-governmental structure, able to solve the collective action problems generated by such situations. The failure is even more stunning as the very nature of the problem recommends a solution based on a polycentric system of government in which different governance units are coordinating under an overarching system of rules and coordinating mechanisms. The European principle of subsidiarity was meant to provide precisely that type of structure.

If we take as a benchmark a functional polycentric system or, more precisely, the idea of a functional polycentric system in which the subsidiarity principle is pivotal, one could easily conclude that in the EU, by 2015 when the crisis started to escalate, the basic conditions of polycentricity were in place. In the case of the EU, the main governance units are the nation states. The EU system provided both an overarching framework and a governance unit aiming to capture externalities transcending the nation states. This system was able to coordinate collective action not only between the states but also between other functional and subnational actors. Obviously they were not perfect, but they definitely were present in a measure larger than in any other significant international governance regime. At least in *de jure* and in theoretical terms, the institutional structure of the EU was polycentric. Its structure and procedural codes satisfied the basic condition of a polycentric system. One could see at work a complex national, regional, local, and supra-national cluster of different decision centers, different jurisdictions working under an overarching system of common rules, given by the EU Constitution and the Acquis communautaire. It is thus fair to presume that the institutional resources to manage the crisis were in place. It is not farfetched to imagine that it was possible, within the existing structures, to have worked out a complex set of possible arrangements and policies, at different levels and calibrated to different circumstances, including between national state and subnational and supra-national entities.

The EU faces its first truly major test in dealing with a crisis of such nature and magnitude. The question is simple: when it comes to the migrant crisis, is the current failure of the EU the result of lack of centralization? Or it is a lack of decentralization and polycentricism? Is it an institutional problem? Or it is a failure to operate correctly within the existing (polycentric) institutional structure?

At one level the answer is straightforward: if the EU was indeed an instance of polycentric system, a failure to the test given by the migrant crisis is a failure of polycentrism. Then the next question is whether that failure is a structural failure, that is to say, a failure derived from the very design or structure of the system. Or does the failure result from the inability of the decision makers to operate the otherwise potentially functional system? What we know from the case so far suggests that we are confronted to the second scenario. A failure due to the inability of decision makers to operate the system is more plausible.

To understand why that is the case, one needs to introduce an additional dichotomy in the picture, one between formal rules and informal rules. At a closer look, at the core of the case is the problem of the differences between the *de facto* and *de jure* rules, between the institutional structure as it is described and prescribed "by the books" as opposed to the ways it is operated "in real life."

The intuitional literature draws attention to the tension between the formal rules of a governance system and the informal relations, arrangements, institutions, and processes that, in fact, dictate the performance of the formal rules. In the case of the EU migrant crisis, the *de facto* operating procedure was not converging with the informal rules. The case shows that despite the *de jure* and formal polycentricity of the system, at least one of the major actors of the system tried to act as if it was operating in a *monocentric* system. We have overviewed the details of the case precisely to give more empirical meaning and consistency to the answer to this puzzle. One of the main insights regarding the systemic failure comes from simply taking a closer look at Germany and its decision makers and their role in all this. The German decision makers operated under an obvious monocentric mindset. They assumed that the weight of Germany in the system was sufficient to offer them the capability of making a monocentric decision. It did not work that way.

The key idea is that polycentric systems are not just structures which once put in place, set into motion automatically institutional solutions to the governance problems encountered. Such systems need to be operating using certain operational codes, values, and attitudes. The stronger the player or decision maker in the system, the more it has to self-regulate in this respect. Structural polycentricism is a necessary condition but not a sufficient one. The structural polycentricism of the European Union was confronted to a crisis, it did not deliver, because the key players did not act as if they were operating in a polycentric system.

In brief, the European migrant crisis offers an insight and a valuable lesson about monocentric and polycentric systems, about state and supra-state actors and their responses in crisis situations. It challenges us to open new venues in the investigation of crises, responses, and governance systems. The approach the Mercatus Center has advanced in the study of the problem of crisis, recovery, and governance arrangements, has been so far the following: start by identifying cases of disasters and crises and the responses to them which are taking place in systems that were operating or were assumed to respond mostly on *centralized, monocentric* principles. Then show through careful case studies the failures in practice and that even in recovery they cannot operate very effectively that way. In cases of real-life crises, these studies have demonstrated that there are many *polycentric, decentralized* local spontaneous responses which are both prompt and effective. The Mercatus approach suggests governance arrangements should allow for more polycentricity and spontaneity. Even in extreme cases such as disasters, the decentralized approach has under-appreciated and under-utilized strengths (Grube and Storr 2014; Storr et al. 2015a, 2015b).

On the other hand, when one turns to the EU migrant crisis, one encounters a different type of case. That is a system which is in theory *polycentric* but once confronted with a crisis, it seems to be unable to practically operate that way. The supra-national polycentric structure is unable to operate as such because in reality it is forced by some major veto players (in this case a major national government) to operate on principles which are alien to a functional polycentric system. The result is a failure in all respects. One obtains neither the polycentric mechanisms, nor the monocentric mechanisms work. The crisis is not solved. It is in fact aggravated.

As mentioned, polycentric structures are a necessary condition for a functional system. But they are not a sufficient one. As any other governance system, polycentricity requires a specific mode of operating. Certain attitudes, expectations, and operational codes are preconditions for the successful functioning of the system. In their absence, a polycentric structure—run on alien principles—may fail or even worse, may collapse. Polycentric systems could be a solution to problems such as the EU migrant crisis. But decision makers have to approach the task of operating such complex systems having the appropriate attitudes and using the adequate operational codes. Power politics and monocentric assumptions and expectations are not among them.

The European migrant crisis is a very interesting and important type of case and as such it (and other similar cases) requires more analysis and evaluation. The major danger looming in such cases is that in the light of failures, there will be voices claiming that one now has living proof of the failure of polycentric governance, a proof that governance under decentralized and subsidiarity arrangements is not feasible in conditions of crisis. Hence more monocentricity and centralization are required. That may be the case. But as far as the existing evidence regarding the current EU developments is concerned, the European migrant crisis is not providing the data and justification to warrant that conclusion.

Notes

1. See also Martin and Zurcher (2008).
2. The Schengen area consists of Belgium, Czech Republic, Denmark, Germany, Estonia, Greece, Spain, France, Italy, Latvia, Lithuania, Luxembourg, Hungary, Malta, the Netherlands, Austria, Poland, Portugal, Slovenia, Slovakia, Finland, and Sweden, along with Iceland, Liechtenstein, Norway, and Switzerland.

References

Archick, K. 2016. The European Union: Current Challenges and Future Prospects. *CRS Report R44249.* Washington, DC: Congressional Research Service. https://fas.org/sgp/crs/row/R44249.pdf.

Greenhill, K.M. 2016. Open Arms Behind Barred Doors: Fear, Hypocrisy and Policy Schizophrenia in the European Migrant Crisis. *European Law Journal* 22 (3): 317–332.

Grube, L.E., and V.H. Storr. 2014. The Capacity for Self-governance and Post-disaster Resiliency. *Review of Austrian Economics* 27 (3): 301–324.

Juchno, P., and M. Agafitei. 2017. Migrant Integration, 2017 Edition. In *Eurostat Statistical Books.* Luxembourg: Publication Office of the European Union. https://ec.europa.eu/eurostat/documents/3217494/8787947/KS-05-17-100-EN-N.pdf/f6c45af2-6c4f-4ca0-b547-d25e6ef9c359.

Martin, P., and G. Zurcher. 2008. Managing Migration: The Global Challenge. *Population Bulletin* 63 (1): 3–20.

Park, J. 2015. *Europe's Migration Crisis.* New York: Council on Foreign Relations. https://www.cfr.org/backgrounder/europes-migration-crisis.

Parkins, J. 2010. Push and Pull Factors of Migration. *American Review of Political Economy* 8 (2): 6–24.

Storr, N.M., E. Chamlee-Wright, and V.H. Storr. 2015a. *How We Came Back: Voices from Post-Katrina New Orleans.* Arlington, VA: Mercatus Center at George Mason University.

Storr, V.H., S. Haeffele-Balch, and L.E. Grube. 2015b. *Community Revival in the Wake of Disaster: Lessons in Local Entrepreneurship.* New York: Palgrave Macmillan.

Tartar, A. 2017. How the Populist Right Is Redrawing the Map of Europe. *Bloomberg,* December 11. https://www.bloomberg.com/graphics/2017-europe-populist-right/.

Thomas, A., and J. Marson. 2018. Germany's Merkel Secures Deal on Migrants, Averts Government Collapse. *The Wall Street Journal,* July 2. https://www.wsj.com/articles/merkel-faces-showdown-over-migrant-policy-1530539359.

Zimmerman, K.F. 1996. European Migration: Push and Pull. *International Regional Science Review* 19 (1–2): 95–128.

Index[1]

A
Adaptation/innovation/adjustment,
    37, 134
Autonomy, 8, 46, 48, 50, 51,
    53–56, 98

B
Business owner(s)/businesses, 2, 4, 5,
    15–17, 20–22, 36

C
Capability, 138
Capacity, 23, 56, 61–83, 111, 135
Centralization, 45–49, 51, 55, 56,
    130, 138, 140
Charities/nonprofits, 5, 22, 35

Children/youth/young people, 2, 4,
    5, 8, 16, 61–83, 96, 116
Citizens, 3, 5, 6, 31, 50, 56, 96, 98,
    99, 102, 122, 132
Civil society, 6, 7, 27–31, 34, 35, 37,
    40, 115
Collective action problem, 3, 5, 7,
    15, 130, 137
Communication, 2, 4, 13, 65
Community, 2–6, 14, 15, 21, 22, 27,
    28, 30, 35, 36, 38, 62, 64, 66,
    69, 79, 80, 98, 102, 111–113,
    115–117, 119–123, 123n1
Complexity, 3, 5, 19, 90
Cooperation, 134
Coordination, 9, 13, 14, 28, 30–34,
    37, 38, 116, 129, 130, 136
Customary/tribal, 113, 115, 117–122

---

[1] Note: Page numbers followed by 'n' refer to notes.

© The Author(s) 2020
S. Haeffele, V. H. Storr (eds.), *Government Responses to Crisis*, Mercatus Studies
in Political and Social Economy, https://doi.org/10.1007/978-3-030-39309-0

D

Decentralization, 7, 38–40, 98, 114, 130, 138
Decision makers/decision making, 7, 15, 23, 51, 89, 94, 116, 131, 135, 138–140
Disaster management, 7, 8, 45–56

E

Earthquakes, 1, 64
Economies of scale, 5, 112, 113
Emergency management (EM), 8, 14, 45–50, 56, 64, 66, 73, 79, 80
Emergency manager(s), 7, 8, 45–56, 73, 79
Entrepreneur(s), 3, 4, 21, 23, 115

F

Famine, 4
Federal/national level, 8, 13, 19, 27–29, 36, 38, 39, 45–48, 50–56, 61–83
Fires, 1, 29, 41n2, 49
Floods, 1, 18, 20, 40
Foreign intervention, 8, 89–106
Funding, 5, 6, 8, 46–52, 54–56, 96, 103

G

Government, 3–8, 13–23, 27–41, 46, 47, 50, 52–56, 64, 69, 79, 80, 83, 84n3, 89, 90, 95, 98, 99, 101, 102, 105, 111–123, 123n1, 135–137, 139
Government official(s), 2, 28, 113

H

Humanitarian/humanitarian aid, 8, 89, 90, 93, 95, 117
Hurricanes, 1, 3, 4, 17

I

Incentives, 4, 8, 14, 29, 32, 91, 96, 98, 101–105, 115, 121, 133
Information, 4, 6, 8, 13, 17, 19, 48, 62, 73, 80, 93, 94, 101, 102, 114, 117
Infrastructure, 4, 5, 90, 95
Institutional reform, 99
Institutions, 8, 27–30, 35, 40, 63, 73, 82, 90–95, 97, 99–103, 112–115, 117–120, 122, 123, 129, 132, 138
Intervention/government intervention, 3, 6–8, 47, 55, 63, 69, 81, 97, 101, 105, 112, 115, 117, 120, 121

K

Knowledge problem, 91–100, 104

L

Local knowledge, 39, 80, 91, 93, 97
Local level, 28, 39, 40, 47

M

Marginalized/vulnerable people/populations, 2–6, 8, 54, 64–66, 69, 82, 83, 123n2, 132, 134

Migrant/immigration/migration, 2, 9, 36, 82, 129–140
Mitigation, 3, 8, 64, 69, 73, 79, 81, 83

N

Natural disasters, 27–41, 47, 64, 122
Natural hazards, 64, 69, 84n2
Networks, 2–4, 69, 73
Norms, 118, 119

P

Partnerships, 73, 116, 117
Policymaker/policymaking, 3, 34, 37, 40, 91
Political economy, 15, 89–106, 114
Political leader(s), 4
Polycentricity/polycentric, 8, 9, 39, 113, 114, 123, 130, 131, 137–140
Preparedness, 3, 8, 14, 47, 48, 50, 54, 62, 63, 65, 66, 69, 73, 79, 80, 83
Private sector, 27–41
Property rights, 16, 17, 20, 37, 38, 90, 91, 114, 118, 122
Public administration, 7
Public goods, 8, 112–116, 120–123
Public sector, 95
Public services, 5, 80

R

Rebuilding, 2–4, 13–23, 37, 82, 90, 102

Recessions/economic downturns, 1–4
Recovery, 3–8, 13–23, 28–30, 33–38, 40, 41, 41n5, 64, 65, 69, 73, 79, 81–83, 100, 139
Resiliency/resilience, 63, 64, 69, 80, 121
Response, 3–9, 13–15, 23, 27–41, 45, 47, 62, 64–66, 69, 73, 79, 80, 82, 83, 90, 94, 96, 111, 112, 115, 117, 120, 122, 129–140
Risk reduction, 64, 73–81, 83
Rules, 6, 7, 14–23, 31–40, 41n3, 41n4, 46, 91, 92, 100–102, 113, 114, 117–119, 122, 130, 137, 138
Rules of the game, 7, 13–23, 28, 31–34, 99

S

Scope and scale, 2, 3, 5, 64
Self-governance, 8, 112, 115, 116, 118, 119, 121, 123
Shortages, 4
Social capital, 4, 6, 30, 116
State-building, 8, 90, 111–123
State level, 52, 129, 134, 136

W

War, 1, 3, 6, 96, 97, 101, 103, 118, 119, 123, 133
Weak states/failed states/weak and failed states, 5, 8, 112, 123

Printed in the USA
CPSIA information can be obtained
at www.ICGtesting.com
LVHW061311060823
754460LV00004B/56